Dance or Die

From Stateless Refugee
to International Ballet Star

A Memoir

Ahmad Joudeh

imagine!

2021 First US Edition

An Imagine Book
Published by Charlesbridge
9 Galen Street
Watertown, MA 02472
(617) 926-0329
www.imaginebooks.net

Originally published as *Danza o Muori,* by Ahmad Joudeh
World copyright © 2018 DeA Planeta Libri s.r.l., Novara

Cataloging-in-Publication Data available upon request.
ISBN 9781623545130 (hardcover) | ISBN 9781632892409 (ebook)

Front and back jacket photographs © Pietro Baroni
Display type set in Alegreya Sans Light
Text type set in Adobe Garamond Pro
Printed by Berryville Graphics in Berryville, Virginia, USA
Production supervision by Jennifer Most Delaney
Jacket design by Cindy Butler
Interior design by Mira Kennedy

Printed in the United States of America
(hc) 10 9 8 7 6 5 4 3 2 1

*I dedicate this book to the spirit that guides every single one of us,
in the memory of the soul, where the flame is, our spirits glow...*

FOREWORD

AHMAD JOUDEH'S STORY is one that is worth knowing, worth recounting to everyone, because it's a story that touches the heart and truly lets us understand the importance of having a dream, of believing in it solidly, and of fighting for it until that dream becomes a reality.

And it's a story that involves me personally and moves me because in some way I'm part of it too.

I met Ahmad for the first time in Amsterdam, in a rehearsal room at the Dutch National Ballet. Over the days leading up to our meeting, I'd heard people talking about him—everyone told me I really had to meet this young man who'd arrived from Syria; I had to hear what he'd been through and how he'd come here. When we were actually face-to-face, Ahmad was full of emotion as he told me his story and how, for him, dancing had come to represent life itself. He also confided to me that I had been a point of reference for him ever since; as a very young child, he had developed a passion for dancing that challenged the prejudices and hostility of his family and social environment. I remained a point of reference in the following years, when he continued to dance despite the outbreak of war and continued to teach dance to children traumatized by the bombs and the violence. These are experiences so difficult and tragic that it's not easy for us even to imagine them.

And yet, even in such an inhuman situation, dance proved to be a redeeming force because art really does have the power to elevate the soul, taking it away from the ugliness and the suffering, and can help us find once more our purest and brightest dimension, the best part of us and of all humanity. It's dance in our case, but it could have been music, poetry, drama—any form of art truly can lead us back into contact with our most authentic essence, with the Absolute.

If this is always true, everywhere, then art's extraordinary power emerges even more clearly in a dramatic story like Ahmad's: its power to provide a positive and completely unexpected turn to existence, even where all hope seems to have been lost. But this can also happen for us, in our society. I think that Ahmad is an example for many young people who all too often are unwilling to fight for their own passions or have difficulty realizing just how many sacrifices; how much dedication, commitment, and determination are necessary for fulfilling our own dreams. Seeking out one's own passion, cultivating it, giving value to it, being ready to face up to the inevitable obstacles in moving forward with it—all this, too, is a lesson that each of us can learn from reading Ahmad's story.

In the end, this story is also emblematic of the drama lived by millions of migrants who are forced to flee from war and violence. Telling this story and letting people know about it allow us to put a human face on the harsh statistics the media transmit to us. The plight of migrants is one that must not be ignored or hidden—it must be known and understood. Especially at this moment in history, it is important to remind ourselves how each of us has a story and carries experiences from which we all can learn.

This is precisely why, in preparing the pas de deux with Ahmad that was broadcast on the Rai Uno television channel in Italy on January 1, 2018, I sought to involve Sting, an extraordinary musician who for some time now, and with great sensibility, has worked for this cause. I wrote to Sting personally to tell him about Ahmad, and even though he was touring at the time, he immediately accepted the job of accompanying us with two of his most unforgettable songs, "Fragile" and "Inshallah."

Sting arranged things so that he arrived in the afternoon, recorded with us, and then left that evening. We had rehearsed very little, but we were determined to give Ahmad the chance of fulfilling another dream and of spreading a message of universal hope. That day, we turned the spotlight on one young person, but there are many like him—each with his or her own experiences, his or her own passions, precisely like Ahmad and like us.

When we finally danced together on television, Ahmad surprised me once more, leaving me amazed at his abilities as he dealt with such a grand and novel situation, a situation he wasn't used to. Once again, he proved he was more than good enough, and his performance went beyond all our expectations. He was professional, self-confident, and in control of his emotions. He was at ease in the element he is made for—dancing. He was in the midst of the impossible dream that he had now transformed into reality.

Roberto Bolle

ONE

IN 1948, AISHA MAWAID was eight years old and living in Saffuriya, near al-Nasrah, in Palestine. She didn't understand why she suddenly had to leave. She was just told that a war had started. "But what is war?" she wanted to know. Her family promised her that they would all return home in a few days' time. There was no need to fret too much. For the moment, however, the only solution was escape.

She took nothing with her; none of her relatives took anything. They left their small family farm and all it contained: a horse, a donkey, the many tools that had been made and accumulated over the years, tools used to work the land that had always fed them. They abandoned the olive trees, the vines, the figs. They didn't even take their gold and their valuables, convinced that they'd find it all intact on their return. They took only some old blankets to keep themselves warm during the cold nights. Before leaving, Aisha took off her favorite earrings. She'd seen the soldiers rip them from the ears of girls of her age. It wasn't the right moment to think too much about what might happen, but the memory of blood and violence and the cries of pain was enough for her to intuit what she had to do to survive.

That same year, the year of the Palestinian exodus during the first Arab-Israeli War, a twelve-year-old boy named Ahmad Joudeh also followed his family's choice of escape. He lived in Lubia, ten kilometers west of Lake Tiberias in the north of Palestine. Following the Israeli victory, he fled to Lebanon. In the chaos he lost his family, but he found them again by pure chance in a refugee camp, and from there they moved together to Syria, settling eventually with other Palestinians on the southern outskirts of Damascus.

Aisha and Ahmad were my grandparents. Fate would bring these two refugees together. When Aisha was in her early twenties, her father wanted her to get married as soon as possible. Though already engaged, she was unsure if her fiancé was the right man for her. When her father showed her a photograph of Ahmad, she saw a handsome man in a policeman's uniform, with a proud and penetrating gaze, vaguely melancholic, with two eyebrows as thick as the mustache above his thin mouth. She looked at the photograph and, partly because he *was* so handsome and partly because of her father's pressure, she simply said yes.

And so my grandparents came to know each other. Aisha joined him in Damascus, where he worked as a traffic policeman, and they got married. It was 1963. She was beautiful, very beautiful, and also very intelligent. She was my grandfather's second wife (multiple marriages were and still are permitted for Muslims in many countries), but she became his favorite and remained so right up to the end. Wafik, my father, was the first born of six boys and three girls.

Theirs was the generation that founded my hometown of Al-Yarmouk. They created it out of an arid and flat no-place on the southern outskirts of Damascus. It was a dead land that over the years filled with people and was transformed into the largest and liveliest Palestinian community in Syria. My family's neighborhood, which over the course of time became a large residential area, looked like a triangle from above, bordered by two wide roads that began in the same square and ran southward, moving diagonally away from each other. One was called Palestine, the other Al-Yarmouk. These two roads were then united by a road that formed the base of the triangle, a road known as Lubia, like the town in which my grandfather was born, now called Lavi. All the roads in the area carried the names of Palestinian towns and cities or Palestinian heroes.

It was a drab neighborhood, made of solid concrete, consisting of high, rectangular blocks interrupted by windows. There were television antennas and cables everywhere, which broke up the monotony of the cubes we lived in. It seemed impossible that all this had been built in the space of a few decades. Al-Yarmouk lay fixed and motionless, timeless, as if it had existed since time immemorial and would exist eternally.

There was no money for making the external walls look pretty, and the only color in the neighborhood was reserved for the schools—blue. It was a gentle and reassuring blue, just slightly darker than the blue of the sky on a sunny day. It was the blue of the United Nations Relief and Works Agency for Palestine Refugees in the Near East (UNRWA), which built schools in our camp and in other camps and areas that housed refugees. But it was also a blue that clashed with the surroundings—it didn't go with the shades of gray, or sometimes beige, of the other buildings; or the light brown of the ground and the dust; or the black of the women who wore hijabs, traditional Muslim veils; or the sober colors of those who didn't wear it. Like my mother, Ramziah.

"Why is the school blue?" I used to ask her.

"Because that way it can't be seen at night and the planes can't bomb it," she would say.

My mother was different from the other women there: free and very strong. She stood up for herself and for other women, and as a teacher she could have run the whole school. When she was twenty-four years old, she gave birth to me, her first male child. The family was so happy, and my grandfather gave me his own name, Ahmad. One year later, she had my brother, Amjad, and after another two years, my sister, Rawan. Our mother worked outside the home and also took care of us at home. We called her "Ram," our supermom.

I grew up in Al-Yarmouk in the 1990s. It was a time of freedom, but also of fear and always of struggle. In my neighborhood, we lived in the open air, everyone together, and the streets were full of people coming and going, or simply standing there to watch the to-ing and fro-ing, seeking out some pastime to make the days go by more quickly.

Every time the Israelis and Palestinians clashed, we heard about it in Al-Yarmouk, and demonstrations would start. I would watch them from on high, up on the roof, lying on my belly: a great seething of restless bodies, a choir of fervent voices, screaming against the violence inflicted, shouting for the land they had unjustly been deprived of, promising revenge, announcing reprisals. Amid the dust from the ground and the smoke from the burning flags, the patriotic songs of our people rose. I knew those songs well, not only because we learned them at school but because I heard them echoing continually, at all hours of the day, through the streets of our quarter.

There was an enemy, this I understood. A cruel enemy that had to be fought. Invisible, but always present. But who were they? What did they look like? In my childish thoughts, homeland, land, and hatred were abstract concepts that I struggled to interpret. What instead was clear to me, because I saw it every day with my own eyes, was that apart from the enemy, there was always something to argue about. There were fights everywhere, throughout the neighborhood. Constantly. Fights would break out for a wrong word spoken, even for just the look on someone's face. Insults and blows would fly; people drew knives, sticks, clubs. From a tender age, I became used to seeing blood flow, and it filled me with terror. This is why, as soon as I could, I would hide on the roof: the world, seen from above, seemed a better place to be. I wanted to be an eagle.

One day, a day like many others, I was up there, admiring the view. The jagged horizon of Al-Yarmouk fascinated me—the irregular roofs, all at different heights, the domes of the mosques, aquamarine or gilded, the minarets, the rusty satellite dishes adding a pleasing touch of red. Gazing slightly farther out, I could make out the center of Damascus, the city. Here too, there were square-shaped and anonymous buildings like mine, with their windows resembling the eyes or nostrils of some strange monster, but there were also small houses nestled between the bigger buildings. How could people live there, I wondered? They must be cramped in such a limited space. Perhaps these people didn't live with their grandparents, their aunts and uncles and cousins, as I did? This seemed impossible to me.

My thoughts were interrupted by a strange noise. Curious, I looked down on my neighborhood and saw a small flock of sheep advancing toward the square where my building stood, the biggest square in Al-Yarmouk. The sheep were coming along Palestine

Road, kicking up a great cloud of dust, surrounded by men who prodded them now and then to keep the laziest on the move. This was an unusual spectacle, so I decided to give it my full attention. I could never have imagined how it was going to end.

Paying no heed to the dust and the gravel, I lay belly down on the roof, my eyes glued to the bizarre scene. When they reached the square, the men tied the sheep to poles planted in the ground. Other men came out of the surrounding houses and shops; they were all talking to one another, rushing up and down, busying themselves with the animals. There was a strange excitement, like an electric current, in the air.

Then there was silence. A big man with a long, black beard arrived from the butcher's shop brandishing a huge knife, as long as his forearm. My heart began beating quickly, and I could feel its pulse against the concrete roof. The butcher approached one of the sheep, kicked it, and pressed its face into the ground with his foot. He called to another man I hadn't seen before and held the knife out to him. The man took it, even though to my terror-filled eyes he seemed slightly hesitant, and shouted, *Bismillah*!—"In the name of God!" He crouched down and with a quick blow cut the sheep's throat. The animal's head bent backward, still attached to its body by the spinal column, as it convulsed, and its blood spurted all over the concrete and mixed with the dust, shining in the afternoon sun.

I wanted to shout, run away, or at least close my eyes, but I couldn't. I was paralyzed by the horror, by my disgust. My muscles had become harder than stone. I remained there, stretched out, prostrate, silent, watching with all the men in the square as the sheep slowly died in what I imagined was terrible suffering. It took at least five minutes for it to stop trembling. And the blood continued to flow, staining the sheep's white coat and the ground.

After returning the knife to the butcher, the man put his hands into the still-warm blood of the poor animal before stamping both palms on a wall, leaving two sinister and bright red handprints. Then he disappeared into the crowd.

The butcher moved a few steps away, grabbed another sheep, and repeated the macabre ceremony: the foot on the animal's face, the knife given to another man, the slash, the blood, the convulsions of the dying body, the death. Then a third sheep, a fourth, a fifth. I counted at least ten before I managed to move, managed to return to my senses. I was shaking and breathing deeply, as though I had just awakened from a bad dream.

"Enough!" I shouted. But with all the fuss down there, no one heard me. The square was littered with corpses. The blood had flowed into every crack in the concrete; it had dirtied the clothes of those present; it had spurted onto the walls. Someone started rinsing the square with buckets of water, creating red rivers that flowed rapidly down Palestine Road, returning along the path that the sheep had taken on the way to their death.

Horrified, I stood up and ran down the stairs. "Enough," I kept saying to myself. I'd decided to confront the butcher. I would speak to him; I would tell him that he was wrong to be so cruel with those poor animals. I had no doubts whatsoever: I would make him see reason, persuade him. Perhaps, upon listening to me, he'd even decide to change jobs! I was so young and naive that his change of heart seemed to me to be perfectly plausible.

The top floor, where my aunt and uncle lived, was empty and quiet. Just as well—I had no desire to meet anyone, no wish to start explaining why I was so upset. I continued down past the other floors, two steps at a time, convinced that no one had noticed me and that I'd be able to complete my mission, when all of a sudden, as I was on the very last flight of stairs, I heard, "Ahmad!"

I had forgotten about my grandmother, who always knew exactly where I was.

"So where have you been?" she asked me, inspecting my dust-covered clothes. "You weren't up on the roof again, were you?"

I didn't answer. I was hoping I could slip away from her, run into the square, and do my duty. But she was a step ahead of me.

"Get a move on. It's time to get washed, otherwise we'll be late," she said, taking me by surprise.

"Late?"

"I knew it. You've forgotten. There's the party this evening, for the wedding of Abd Alaziz and Mohammad's daughter. The whole neighborhood's going to be there, and we of all people have to be there."

The wedding! So that was the reason for the massacre I'd witnessed. Suddenly it was all clear to me, and yet I still felt upset. OK, the sheep had been slaughtered for a wedding feast, but was all that cruelty really necessary? Couldn't the butcher at least have stroked them before killing them, rather than kicking them? And now I realized the identity of the man was who'd killed the first sheep: the groom, Abd. But how could his wife love a person capable of such cruelty? (As a child, I didn't know that it was an act of tradition for the groom to kill the first sheep—as evidence of his prosperity and strength.)

Sulking, I followed my grandmother back into our house. The door behind us remained ajar. This had been one of her ideas, and I'd stopped wondering about it: she'd had all the locks and bolts in the house—the main door and those of all the rooms—set up so that the doors were always at least ajar, if not wide open. It was a good example of my grandmother's own openness.

In my room, I took my clean clothes—the finest, my sugar-feast clothes—and headed toward the bathroom. My grandmother was waiting for me in the corridor, to make sure that I didn't try to escape.

"Granny Aisha," I said. "I saw them kill the sheep."

"Ah, yes?"

"It was terrible, the most disgusting thing in the world. Why did they kill them like that? They hadn't done anything to anyone!"

She put a hand to my head, stroked my hair. She was late, and it was my fault, and she was probably angry, but her voice remained full of sweetness, as always. "Do you remember last week, when I made that stew for you?" she said. "You had three platefuls, if I remember well. You kept saying you wanted more, said it was very good. You know what was in it, don't you?"

I stood there for a moment with my mouth open and then turned my eyes to the floor.

"Exactly, there was mutton in there. And the raw chicken liver you love so much? That too comes from an animal. An animal that was slaughtered so that you can eat it."

There was no way out. I had no idea what to say; nothing intelligent came to mind. So I simply said the first thing that came into my head: "There was no need for them to kill a sheep for me, because I certainly won't be eating any after everything I've seen."

"No problem, fine, don't eat sheep. But hurry up now—before long, your grandfather will be back home, and you don't want him to see you in this state. Go get washed, come on!"

Before returning to her chores, she gave me a smile, and I saw that she was a little proud of my stubbornness.

As I was going into the bathroom, my Uncle Omar shouted from his room, "Ahmad! Ahmad!" I went to him and saw him on his mattress on the floor, as usual—as usual because he was completely paralyzed from his neck to his knees; he couldn't bend his hips or his back.

"Ahmad, I need to piss now!" he said, a big smile stretched across his face.

My uncle needed all sorts of attention that kept us all busy, and we helped out because it was impossible not to love him and because he himself had a heart of gold. Generous and really funny, he always managed to find an excuse for laughing about everything, even about his own condition. In this case, my job was to turn him on his side, undo his trousers, put the chamber pot in position, and turn my eyes elsewhere. When he'd finished, I would empty the pot, and I was free. Through helping Uncle Omar, I grew up with the belief that I should help and take care of others with love.

"So, what have you been up to today?" he asked while relieving himself.

"Nothing much," I said. "I saw them getting things ready for the wedding this evening." Then I told him all about the sheep.

"I could hear the noise even in here. It'll be a great party, no doubt. There'll be plenty to eat, to drink, and then music and dancing. You'll have a good time, I'm sure."

But I wasn't sure at all.

He nodded at my torn trousers and dirty knees. "You've been on the roof watching the preparations, no? You can't imagine how much I'd like to come up there with you. But don't worry, I won't say anything—I know you like being up there on your own, with no one disturbing you. But if I could, I swear I'd run up those stairs just to sit in silence with you."

I leaned over to kiss and hug him, and I promised that I would carry him to the roof when I grew up. His kindness never failed to astonish me. I knew that Uncle Omar was one of the few people who really understood me.

"But get a move on now—you don't want to get your grandmother angry, do you?"

AN HOUR LATER, fresh and clean, I finally went down into the square, wearing a perfectly ironed white shirt. Not a trace of the afternoon's slaughter remained, and I wondered for a moment whether it had just been a nightmare. And the spectacle before me now took my breath away: colored garlands hanging from one side of the square to the other, together with strings of lights giving off a warm and gentle glow that glinted off the plates and silverware on the many tables. At least a hundred chairs had been brought into the square for the occasion, with as many more on their way. I could smell a subtle aroma of spices that made my mouth water—nothing like the terrible smell of blood just a few hours earlier.

Before I had a chance to take in that incredible scene fully, I was surrounded by a bunch of excited kids, including my younger sister, Rawan, and my cousins, all fifteen of them, who bombarded me with questions and demands:

"Ahmad, come here!"

"Finally, you've arrived! Look over there—the kids from the school are here too."

"No, wait! Let's take him to see the musicians first. Look, Ahmad, your dad's with them."

They pulled me by my hand and my shirt in every direction. But I managed to calm their excitement by exercising the responsibility and the authority of the eldest, which they respected. In truth, even though I was reluctant to admit it, I was beginning to feel slightly hungry.

"Shall we go eat something first?" I said. "What do you say?"

My cousins always responded to my proposals with joy. Jumping, running, and shouting, we crossed the square and headed for the main banquet table. Without my even having to ask for it, a woman handed me a plate of meat in a paprika sauce. It was warm and smelled delicious, but I only ate the sauce.

"My dad cooked it," said one of my many cousins, proudly.

"They brought the sheep in this afternoon. You should've been there, Ahmad; there was blood everywhere. It was awesome!"

I didn't answer. I was trying not to vomit.

"Do you want the meat?" I said, holding out my plate to one of my cousins. "I'm not really that hungry."

He gobbled it up in an instant, while I continued to struggle to keep down the little food I had eaten. As soon as he'd finished, we started playing. I ran up and down the square, my cousins following me, running among the guests, dodging chairs, passing through the legs of the grown-ups, under the tables, as a little dog joined us, barking. I dealt with my hunger and upset stomach with a handful of sweets that I grabbed from a tray. I was eight years old, and soon my worries flew away in a rush as I did my best to enjoy myself.

I led the gang to the musicians in the center of the square. They were tuning their instruments while in front of them a group of men, hand in hand in a circle, prepared to do the *dabka*, a frenetic, joyous dance marked by acrobatic jumps and quick steps, with the first in line swinging a rope or a handkerchief in the air with his free hand.

Someone grabbed my arm and abruptly stopped my running— it was my father.

"Here, take it," he said, putting a microphone into my hand. It always ended up like this at weddings, or at any occasion where there was an audience to entertain. My father, who taught both music and painting, said that I had a fine voice and absolutely had to sing, accompanied by my brother, Amjad, who played the oud, a type of guitar that originally comes from Persia.

Amjad was already there, alongside our father, his eyes on the ground and an air of melancholy in his expression that never left him. I didn't understand my brother and really didn't know him that well. The only thing we had in common was music. We didn't even live together; I lived with my grandmother and he lived a few floors up, with our parents.

"But Wafik," one of the musicians protested to my father, "we already have a singer."

"Just let my boys do a couple of songs. They'll amaze you all."

My brother, in silence, went over to the oud player and took the instrument from his hands, not rudely but decidedly. He sat next to me, and we immediately began with a number from our repertoire. The dancers let go of each other's hands; some of them moved away while others sat down to listen, a little annoyed by this change to the program but pleasantly surprised when they heard us. I did have a good voice, and my brother was an excellent oud player.

It was a nice moment: the warm light, almost red, of the sunset; the many decorations hanging above our heads; the evening breeze cooling the sweating faces; and the music cradling us all, even those who paid no attention.

Suddenly, from the other side of the square, came the growing noise of raised voices, which soon escalated into shouting. People stopped listening to us and ran to see what was happening. Left with no audience, Amjad and I followed them to the shouting and the rising dust. There was a fight going on. A brawl, and it was difficult to say how many people were involved. It took place right outside my Uncle Hisham's real estate agency, which had been transformed into a bar for serving coffee to the wedding guests. And Hisham was in the middle of the brawl, with another of my uncles, Abid.

Hisham was the director of the agency. He'd left school at the age of nine and didn't know how to read or write, but this didn't seem to be a problem for him at work. Of all my uncles, he was the most handsome, the most elegant, and the best dancer. Abid, on the other hand, was easily recognized by his unsteady gait. He was almost always drunk, and even when sober he was always confused, and yet he was the kindest of them all. He often argued with my other uncles because of his alcoholism. The truth is that everyone in the neighborhood enjoyed a drink, but Abid did more than most.

My uncles were trying to calm down two men laying into one another. Other men had joined the melee, and there was so much confusion that you couldn't really understand who was fighting whom. Getting closer to the brawl, I could make out a few phrases here and there:

"Just leave my sister alone!"

"It's not my fault if you lock her away in the house. Of course she goes to the window to look at the men."

"Don't you tell me what to do!"

"And don't you tell me where to look!"

I was used to such scuffles, and I knew that this one wouldn't peter out until all those involved had fallen to the ground, their energy spent. And these fights had a tendency to grow: when the men who stepped in to try to break it up were dealt random blows, they got mad and joined in the brawl, which continued to get bigger and bigger.

After all I had witnessed—the killing of the sheep, the sudden outburst of violence—my eight-year-old heart was filled with disgust. I loved beauty: music, dance, the mountains in the distance. Here we were, gathered to celebrate a wedding, the coming together in love of two people within our community, and these men were spoiling it with violence.

My uncles had their flaws, but they were strong and brave. Many times they had rushed to our aid, protecting us from the dangers of the streets. I liked them, and I wanted to help them stop the fight.

I had an idea. I gathered my cousins together, all of them excited by what was happening. "Guys, come over here," I said. "We'll show them now. Follow me!"

With a long trail of children behind me, I plunged through the wall of grown-ups beating each another up, reached the door of our building, and climbed to the first floor.

"Everyone grab a container, as big as possible. Those who live here, get them from your houses, and get another one for the others. Fill them with cold water, and then run up to where I'll be, on the roof. Understood?"

"Yessss!" the chorus replied, full of adrenaline.

I went into our apartment and grabbed a couple of saucepans. As I was about to leave, I remembered Uncle Omar's chamber pot. I went into his room. He was awake and watching television.

"Uncle, can I take your pot? It's for something urgent. I'll explain later."

"My pot? Why do you want that?"

"I just do."

He seemed to guess what I was up to and went along with my plan. "OK. If you really need it . . . but before you do, let me empty my bladder, please," he said with his usual smile.

"But of course," I said, with an even bigger smile.

I waited for him to finish, lifted the pot, and joined my sister and my cousins.

There we were, seventeen of us altogether, each with a container full of water in our hands, plus Uncle Omar's special container. We climbed to the roof and looked down on the fighting. The sun had set, and in the growing darkness, it was difficult to make anything out. The mass of men fighting was like a monster writhing, its thousand arms thrust in every direction, kicking up dust that rose toward us, making it even harder to see. I so wanted to stop the fighting.

"Right," I told the kids. "We'll send down three waves of water, five saucepans at a time. There's no point trying to take aim, just throw it at the group and just hope we hit the mark." I counted down: "Three . . . two . . . one . . . water!"

The first wave of five saucepans' worth of water fell on the men and the dust, which now turned into muddy dirt after mixing with water and fell on the men. With their eyes full of dirt, their punches were now being thrown blind.

"Another five, quickly!" I said.

With the dust settled, we could see better and could be more precise. The second wave was much more effective—the brawlers, soaked now, quickly moved away to avoid another shower. But the strongest, or the most furious, stood their ground, including my uncles. Suddenly I recognized someone else—it was the butcher who had killed the sheep that afternoon. I recognized the way he moved and his long, thick beard. I saw my chance to avenge those poor animals whose throats he'd cut.

"Three . . . two . . . one . . . piss!"

The last wave rained gloriously down, putting an end to the violence. Uncle Omar's chamber pot I had aimed at the butcher, hitting my mark. He pulled up his shirt, sniffed it, and made a face.

While my cousins and I were busy laughing and cheering over our achievement, someone down there finally realized we were up on the roof and started shouting at us. Those who recognized their sons shouted up with the worst threats, while the others made do with a barrage of generic insults. We decided to disperse so as to attract less attention. My sister and my cousins ran downstairs and mixed with the crowd as though nothing had happened.

I stayed up on the roof to enjoy the view from above. I lay down on the concrete, satisfied, not even worrying about dirtying my good clothes. The party was already underway again—the voices coming up were full of joy and cheerfulness. The music, the lights, a drunk in the corner heading off home swaying this way and that, perhaps leaning on a shoulder belonging to someone he'd been fighting with just a few minutes ago. That was Al-Yarmouk—chaotic, but united in a common destiny that the daily fights couldn't diminish. I had achieved my goal: stopping violence; returning to my culture's celebration and to beauty.

But even at eight years old, I knew I was somehow different. I lifted my eyes and imagined an escape, allowing myself to soar away from the party, like an eagle, beyond the roofs and the minarets, beyond even the city of Damascus, with its lights and shadows, all the way to the massive dark outline of Mount Qasioun, with its foothills shining with the lights of tiny houses and its ridge climbing toward the summit, challenging the sky, a ridge that ran toward a moon that bathed the sky in its light and made it shine, as if made of silver.

Two

EVEN LIVING IN A neighborhood of refugees, the youth of Al-Yarmouk had opportunities to practice the arts. The Al-Maqdisi theater in Damascus would organize occasional shows in collaboration with the schools in the city. We, the Al-Yarmouk students, were selected once. Everyone did whatever they were best at: some acted; some read their own writing and poetry; some danced the dabka, a folk dance; and some, like my brother and me, played music or sang.

Our parents always attended when we performed, especially our father, who was our artistic mentor. He had taught us everything about art and always pushed us to do our best. He would get us anything that in his opinion might help us improve—musical instruments or a good stereo for listening to the works of great composers, music stands, sheet music, and microphones. In addition to music, my father made us draw and paint, and he would buy us easels, canvases, paints, brushes, and paper.

So art was welcome in our house, even though it was often more of a duty than a pleasure. It was also the thing that united us more than anything, because up to the age of fourteen I lived with my grandparents and was brought up by them. Music and drawing were the only opportunities for interaction with my father, my brother, and my sister, and they were precious to me. But these interactions were also complicated, especially with my father. On the one hand, he was very supportive; on the other, his harsh personality and set ideas about what boys should and shouldn't do would, over time, create a great barrier between us.

At Al-Maqdisi, I looked out from behind the curtain—the theater was full, with at least a hundred people, perhaps more. This wasn't the first time we'd performed for such a big audience, so we were quite relaxed, except for that slight pang in the stomach that always got me just before I went on stage. But my father was frightened; he was very nervous backstage and kept running around, with my mother and my sister looking on in exasperation.

"Do you remember the lyrics, Ahmad?" he asked me. My brother had chosen a poem from his schoolbook and made a song of it, which I was to sing accompanied by him on the oud and our little sister on the keyboard.

"Yes, Dad."

"Get it, go through it again."

"He's told you he remembers it, Wafik. Stop bothering him," my mother said.

"Don't interfere. And you, Amjad, are you sure of the music? Make sure you don't change the arrangement at the last minute. And stop looking out from behind that curtain—you're the entertainment, not the audience! Concentrate!"

Before us on the agenda was a group of kids who danced the dabka. I liked watching them. Whenever I saw anyone dancing, I was really caught up in it and felt the need to move in time with them, even if it was only some little move or keeping the rhythm with my foot. But my father hated it when I concentrated on something else, and he would become really impatient.

"Ahmad, please, just think about what you have to do and nothing else. Your schoolmates' families are out there in the audience—you don't want to make a bad impression on them, do you?"

He had a stern look on his face—he wasn't really asking a question. When the dancers who came before us were just about to finish, one of the organizers came over to us and whispered, "There's a problem . . . the microphone's not working."

I had always sung with a microphone, and my father was well aware of this. This technical hitch threatened to undo all of his plans.

"So, do you want to go ahead anyway? Shall I present you or not?" the organizer asked insistently.

"Ahmad, you'll have to sing as loudly as you can," my father said, his face very serious and more determined than ever. He nodded to the organizer, who told us to follow him. We walked together, and then he left my brother and me standing behind my father in the wings.

We were presented, took our positions under the lights in the middle of the stage, and started our performance. It was strange, singing without a microphone. I much preferred directing my voice toward an object rather than pulling it out of me and letting it fly freely through the auditorium. But I had no other choice, and so I tried my best. And it went well: at the end of the song, we received waves of applause. The audience was happy, which meant we'd done our duty, and after a quick bow I could return backstage with relief. Our father was also pleased with our performance and even gave us a brief nod and a curt, "Well done."

We left the backstage area together, walking quickly to catch the last bus for Al-Yarmouk. I was the last in line, and I was thinking about how it would be nice to sit in the theater and watch the other kids' performances instead of having to run off and lock ourselves away at home. All of a sudden, a noise caught my attention. In truth, it wasn't really a noise—it was music, a music that I had never heard before. I looked at my family, just a few steps in front of me, but my curiosity got the better of me, and I slipped away through the first door on the right, which led directly into the auditorium. And I was dumbfounded by what I saw.

On stage were six girls dressed in purple and black, moving in perfect harmony with one another and with that strange melody accompanying them. They were rapid and elegant in their movements, full of grace, and they moved their bodies in a way that was unknown to me.

Their slender legs, rendered even more shapely by their tights, drew wide arcs in the air and reached heights that I would have thought impossible. And their feet? Ah . . . there they are! They were hidden in strange shoes that had soles where the toes were rather than on the bottom of the foot, which meant they could stand on tiptoe as if without effort. Their backs were so elastic that their torsos flexed backward vertiginously; their arms, long and tapered, seemed to me to be as elegant as a swan's wings I had seen in cartoons; their hands caressed the air to the rhythm of the music.

And they were so beautiful. As they wove across the stage, these girls smiled, full of concentration but happy, as though it was all effortless. Their bodies were feathers, and the wind made them dance to its music.

I was enchanted by this wonderful spectacle, and I sat in the dark near the door where I had entered. I wished it would never end—I had never felt such peace before in all my life. Instinctively, I began to move my head and my back in waves, as the dancers were doing. I felt free and weightless, guided not by my thoughts but by the increasingly compelling music.

I didn't see the door open and my father's head appear as he searched for me in the auditorium. But I did feel his strong, rough hand as it grabbed my arm and dragged me away from that enchantment.

"What do you think you're doing?" he asked, slamming the door shut, unworried about disturbing the show. "Come on, get a move on! We're all waiting for you. And now, because of you, we have to walk—we've missed the last bus."

I didn't care if my father was angry, or if we had to walk home now, or if I would be punished the next day. I felt as though I'd just woken from the sweetest of dreams, and I couldn't think about anything else. My eyes didn't register the road before me or my father's furious face. All I could see were six ballerinas on a stage, moving in unison. I was overwhelmed.

"What was that music?" I asked.

"Tchaikovsky," came his irritated reply.

"And what's the song called?"

"*Swan Lake*. And it's not a song, it's a symphony."

Swans. So I was right, the ballerinas really had moved like swans. It wasn't by chance.

"Could you get the record of the symphony? I'd like to hear all of it."

"Yes, all right. But for now, just shut up and walk. Walk this slowly and we'll never get home."

After that, I didn't have the courage to ask him anything else. I'd have liked to know much more, especially about the ballerinas' dancing, but something told me that it was best not to talk about it.

My father never did bring me a recording of *Swan Lake*. I had to turn to my mother.

"It's called ballet, or classical dance," she replied.

"And why have you never mentioned it to me?"

"Because you can't be interested in it—it's a woman's thing."

But when we arrived home, I couldn't get the dancers' image out of my head. I went to my room, locked the door, and started imitating them and dancing like them, which became my secret daily prayer.

RELIGION WAS ANOTHER regular part of our lives in Al-Yarmouk, though we certainly weren't the most devout of families. We didn't always fast; not all of the women wore hijabs; and, as I've mentioned, my uncles drank a bit too much. Despite all this, in common with most Muslims, we went to the mosque every Friday. I often went there with my grandfather. For him, it was very important to let me hear the prayers and the words of the adults. He would tell me that there was always something to learn, from anyone, even from those with whom I didn't agree. And then, on the way home, we would talk. He would ask me questions and wanted me to respond, even if sometimes his questions were really difficult for a nine-year-old child.

I would hold on to the sleeve of his jacket (he never really felt like wearing a *gallabia*, a traditional Muslim robe) and almost had to run to keep up with him, just as my mind had to race to understand the complexity of his questions. Sometimes I really didn't know what to say; certain things were too profound, too far from my daily life, and yet I was never intimidated by them. My grandfather did everything possible to keep me at ease, and he listened to me with full respect, whatever I said. These thinking exercises that he put me through made me grow up quickly—by treating me as an adult, my grandfather made me one.

He was well known for his judgment and his integrity. In 1956, around the time of the Suez Crisis, the Syrian president Shukri Al-Quwatli issued an order limiting the use of cars in Syria in order to provide fuel to support the Egyptian people. As a traffic policeman, my grandfather was responsible for upholding this law. One day, a car he stopped for violating the order actually carried President al-Quwatli. The president said to my grandfather, "I am Shukri Bey, president of the republic." My grandfather replied, "Even if you are the president of the republic, an order is an order." The president smiled and accepted the traffic ticket. The next day, the president sent my grandfather a gift, along with the honor of an invitation to the president's office.

Because of my grandfather's wisdom and experience, many people sought his advice and approval. One Friday, after our usual visit to the mosque, he had some visitors, and he asked me to stay with him rather than going to see my cousins. It was a privilege reserved for me because I was his eldest grandchild; I could be introduced to the adults and serve them coffee, even when they were meeting to discuss important matters. They also appreciated his coffee, the best in the neighborhood. He made it himself, buying the beans when they were still fresh and green, leaving them to dry, and then roasting them, breaking them up, and grinding them—by which time everyone in the building and beyond knew that it was the right moment to visit him. Every morning, he made enough coffee to fill a big thermos flask that lasted all day, so that anyone who dropped in could help themselves without feeling they were imposing.

The walls of the living room of my grandparents' house were covered with plates and cups hung on hooks. Normally, we kids weren't allowed to touch them, but that day was different, at least for me. My grandfather chose three cups of white porcelain, finely decorated with flowers and inscriptions, and he gave them to me before leaving to get ready to receive his friends.

I went to the kitchen with these treasures in my hands, and in my mind I went over my task, afraid that I might forget something. The coffee ceremony, in our house, was a ritual with very precise laws. The guests had to be served clockwise, and if anyone shook their cup, that meant that I wasn't to fill it again. The cups were to remain on the table at the end of the visit. When I heard voices from the other room, I knew my moment had arrived. I took the three cups in my left hand and the long and heavy thermos in my right, as tradition required, and headed to the living room.

My grandfather had washed and changed and was now wearing a wide-fitting beige shirt and equally wide trousers. With him were two men I'd never seen before: the first wore a gray robe to his ankles and a red and white *kaffiyeh* around his shoulders; the second had on a red waistcoat decorated with geometric patterns over a white shirt, black trousers, and a small white hat on his bald head. All three were sitting cross-legged on the floor, before the table.

"This is Ahmad, Ahmad Joudeh," my grandfather said, introducing me. "He carries the same name as me and some coffee for all of us."

"Hello, little one," the man in the kaffiyeh said. "Your grandfather often talks of you; he says you're already a smart young man."

I replied modestly, as I had been taught: a little smile and a nod of the head, no more. I served the coffee and sat in a corner while the guests chatted of this and that. The first round was followed by a second, and then a third, but the conversation remained at the level of small talk—the heat, a little politics, some childhood memories, but no more. I started feeling a bit disappointed—my grandfather had promised they'd be talking about important things that day, and I was very curious.

At a certain point, I realized that *I* was the problem. I noticed that the guests were exchanging some meaningful looks, and I started sweating. I didn't know what to do—leaving the room would have been the right thing to do, but I couldn't leave until one of them asked me explicitly to do so.

After another quarter of an hour of chatter, the man with the kaffiyeh finally made up his mind. "We have to talk now, Ahmad. Ask your grandson to leave. Off you go, little one, and thanks for the coffee. Actually, just leave it here and we'll take care of it."

An adult's request should always be respected, whatever that request may be. So even though I was sorry to go, I was about to put the thermos on the table and leave the room.

But my grandfather had a different opinion. "Stay here, Ahmad. Sit down here next to me and listen. There is nothing, gentlemen, that we cannot talk about in the presence of my grandson. He's much more intelligent and grown up than he seems."

If an adult's request was an order for me, then my grandfather's was law, for everyone. His guests didn't reply, and even if there was a certain disapproval in their eyes, the conversation they'd come to our house to have could finally begin.

"It's about my son," said the man with the kaffiyeh, "and his wife. Things aren't going well between them, and they're thinking about divorce."

"Really? And what makes you think that might be the best choice?" my grandfather asked.

"It's his wife's fault—she doesn't treat him properly. She's grown old too quickly and seems to be a different person compared to the woman she was before they married. And she still hasn't given him a child!"

"Have you spoken with her about this?"

"Of course, and she doesn't accept any of it—she says she's a good wife, she runs the house well . . . and she's right about that, but that's not enough."

"However, to tell the whole story," his friend in the waistcoat interrupted timidly, "there's something else—she complains because, in her words, her husband 'isn't man enough.'"

"That's not true! My son is the manliest man in Damascus. He's a bricklayer and spends all day every day lifting tons of cement under the sun. You should see the muscles in his arms."

The man was clearly upset, his pride probably hurt. He vented his anger for a few minutes before my grandfather spoke again.

"Listen," my grandfather said when the man had finished. "I built this house myself, with my own hands, and I am still building it. I built one floor after another for each of the families of my children, and one day Ahmad too will help me build his apartment."

Hearing my name suddenly mentioned made me jump, so taken was I with the discussion. I turned toward my grandfather, who gave me a fond smile before continuing. "Now, in your opinion, am I still in the prime of my strength? Do I look to you like a fiery and passionate young man?"

The man with the kaffiyeh lowered his eyes with an embarrassed look. I'm not sure he knew what my grandfather was getting at, while I, knowing my grandfather very well, began to intuit something. The man replied cautiously, trying to change the subject, "But no, Ahmad, what's that got to do with it? We are old now; you can't make these comparisons."

"Exactly, you can't make these comparisons. What I want to say is that muscles are not a sign of virility, just as building a house is not a sign of it. If necessary I can be a bricklayer, and yet I'm no longer able to satisfy a woman. It's not enough to work on a building site to be a real man."

A real man. My grandfather emphasized the last three words of his discourse, and I felt a shiver down my back. Muscles weren't enough to be a real man; lifting concrete wasn't enough. What is *a real man*? Someone like my grandfather, certainly. And my father. But me? Would I ever become *a real man*?

The man with the kaffiyeh looked at the floor, as though following the patterns in the carpet we were sitting on. With his legs crossed, his hands held together around his ankles, he sighed deeply before asking, "So? What should we do?"

"Don't ask me; ask him," my grandfather replied, indicating me with a nod of his head.

The man's eyes opened wide and his mouth fell open, his gaze shifting from my grandfather to me. He was upset; he couldn't believe what my grandfather had just said. And he was angry.

"*Him*? You're telling me to talk to a nine-year-old about my problems?" He ran his hand across his sweat-covered forehead and then, lowering his voice, he whimpered, "Why are you doing this to me, Ahmad? Are you making fun of me? Humiliating me right now when I need help?"

"I would never show you such disrespect, you must know that," my grandfather replied, keeping calm. "I'm just telling you to ask my grandson because I know that he has the answer and I know it's the same as the answer I would give you. Come on, Ahmad, tell him . . . what should they do?"

If at that moment a great hole had opened up in the floor, ready to swallow me up, I would have gladly dived into it, just to disappear. I could feel the man's angry gaze, and there was no way I wanted to make him any angrier. But at the same time, I didn't want to disappoint my grandfather, who expected a lot from me. I rubbed my nose nervously with my hand, and then, without lifting my eyes from the floor, said in a single breath, "Divorce is a valid option, but more for her than for him. If, as the woman says, your husband is not enough of a man, then the fault lies with your son, who isn't respecting his conjugal duties, and this is why they have no children yet. You should be grateful that this woman is still there, carrying out her tasks without asking for anything in return. This means she truly loves her husband."

I had said what I knew to be the truth from listening to my grandfather over time. A profound silence filled the room. The man with the kaffiyeh began looking at the carpet. My grandfather instead stared at the ceiling and seemed to be deep in thought. Not knowing what to do, my cheeks red with shame, I poured more coffee into their empty cups and sat down, hoping the visit would end as soon as possible. And that's exactly what happened.

The man with the kaffiyeh was the first to get up, followed by his friend in the waistcoat. They took their leave quickly but politely. I imagine they were embarrassed at the idea of a child revealing such an obvious truth to them, so obvious that it was clear to everyone—they hadn't been able to see it only because they were blinded by pride.

"*Assalamu alaykum*, thank you for your advice." And then, turning to me, "Your grandfather is right, you're too smart for your age. Keep it up and you'll achieve great things in life."

"*Wa alaykum assalam*, thank you for coming; it is always a pleasure to see you."

I took refuge in the kitchen while my grandfather accompanied them to the door and there, finally on my own, I started breathing again. While I was at the sink, busy washing the cups, my grandfather joined me. My nerves, stressed by the afternoon I'd just had, relaxed with a shiver of relief when I heard him say: "He's right. Keep it up and you'll achieve great things, Ahmad."

EVERYTHING, GOOD OR BAD, must come to an end. And that is a hard lesson for a twelve-year-old child to learn.

The sun had set two hours ago, but from the open window came a warm, delicate breeze that filled the room. I wasn't asleep yet, and sleeping was the last thing on my mind. I just wanted to lie there on my bed, staring at the ceiling, hoping to be able to stop time and make that night last forever.

I closed my eyes and began to dig into my memories, searching for remembrances to keep alive.

A simple melody was the first thing to come to me, and it played insistently in my head. Then came instruments and voices until it transformed into a song. I concentrated to recall the lyrics:

> *O mulberry of my home, be patient, even if life*
> *oppresses you*
> *We'll surely be back, no matter how long the journey*
> *O waters, be calm, we've been away so long, greet the*
> *land on which we grew*
> *Greet the olive trees and the family that raised me…*

The voice belonged to the Palestinian singer Abu Arab, my grandfather's favorite singer, and the song was "Hadi Ya Bahar Hadi." (Oh, sea waters be calm.) An image took shape in my mind: smoke, curling gently in the air, little vortices that rose and dissolved; a cigarette in a holder made of light-colored wood, the holder held in a mouth that had spoken so often to me and to which I had listened so respectfully. It was my grandfather, sitting on the floor, his legs crossed, smoking in front of the television, listening to this song.

Then, another image—a sepia-colored photograph, hanging on the wall of the kitchen, of my grandfather as a young man. He was wearing his policeman's uniform, with its lapels, its epaulettes, and its shiny silver buttons; he was even wearing his official hat, a tall one with a short visor and a shining coat of arms at its center. His face, as always, was perfectly shaved, apart from the thick and tidy mustache above lips that were closed but slightly raised in the beginnings of a smile. Above the mustache his big, significant nose sat between his small eyes with their intense, direct, and, when necessary, severe gaze. Next to my grandfather was my grandmother, beautiful as ever.

But my grandmother at that moment was asleep in the next room, and I had no need to remember her. My grandfather, his body lying alongside me, merited all my thoughts.

From his side, a sharp, unnatural chill began to rise, mixed with the warm air coming from the window. I took the ice blocks that lay between me and him and put them on the other side, to his right. It was only a matter of hours now—the night would soon end, and then they would come to take him away.

I didn't want to accept that he had gone, but I knew I had to, now, before they buried him. Lying on my side, I observed his motionless and silent body. With my eyes, I caressed his profile, the profile I knew so well. Stupidly, I was convinced that he could hear me, so I searched my mind for something significant to say to him. But I found nothing. Nothing new, at least; nothing I had not already told him. Perhaps in death my grandfather had taken my intelligence with him. Perhaps now, without him, I wouldn't be the same as before. Or, perhaps more likely, no words were needed in that moment—words never were of any use with him, the man who knew how to read me inside out, even when I was silent.

I thought again of the things my grandfather had taught me: how to speak, how to reason, how to behave in the midst of people. Apart from music and drawing, everything I knew came from him. I realized then that he had been my true father, and I had just lost him. That night helped me understand this fact, to accept it. And it helped me resign myself to having to survive without him. Now I was Ahmad Joudeh, and no one else was. I had to honor the name we had shared, and I had to be proud of the responsibility this involved.

I took his hand and shivered from its cold, but his lifeless body didn't frighten me. I turned toward the window—far off, I could see the first glow of dawn. I was ready to sleep, finally. I was so tired that I didn't wake up, even when they came to take him. I held his hand firmly while a tear, the first and last tear of that night, ran down my cheek toward the pillow. Like my tear, I too was alone.

THREE

"LET'S START FROM THE TOP. Ahmad, concentrate. And three and four and . . . "

My brother started playing the piano again. It was a piece we'd been practicing for more than an hour in the living room of my parents' house. My father was there as usual, directing our performance, but in that rehearsal, he started losing his patience after a little glitch cropped up. That glitch was me.

After eight beats of the introduction, I was to start singing, and that's exactly what I did. But that day, my voice was not what it usually was.

"Ahmad, please, that's enough now! Are you doing this deliberately? Once again . . . go!"

My voice was hoarse. I struggled to reach the high notes—my voice just wasn't up to it and kept cracking suddenly. I'd never experienced anything like this; it had just appeared out of the blue. I blamed a cookie that I'd eaten just before at my grandmother's, because that was precisely the sensation: sharp crumbs sticking in my throat, moving around and scratching every time I tried to go up the scale.

I stopped singing and tried to explain to my father what was happening. Both he and my brother gave me stern looks: Amjad seemed somehow satisfied, while my father was furious.

"Are you telling me this rehearsal is a waste of time because you have a sore throat?"

"Yes . . . but it's not a sore throat. It's just a feeling . . . "

"So what is it then?"

He was beginning to frighten me—his nostrils had widened, and he was drumming his fingers vigorously on the table he was leaning on. I concentrated on the rhythm of his fingers just to stop myself from being overwhelmed by the sobbing I could feel welling up in my chest.

"I can't sing the high notes. My voice is stuck."

"What do you mean, 'stuck'? You can talk, can't you? And you've been singing. Singing badly, but you've been singing. So how can you say you've lost your voice?"

"Yes, but I can't . . . "

Behind him, sitting at the piano, my brother was enjoying a good snicker.

"What is it you can't do? Up until yesterday, you were singing perfectly, now you suddenly say you can't manage? If you're trying to pull my leg, it's a dangerous game you're playing."

My father was now standing before me and shouting directly in my face. His neck was flushed, and its veins were bulging. I kept my gaze fixed on the floor, at a point between his feet and mine, which made him appear even taller and more threatening. I couldn't say anything because even opening my mouth to breathe would have meant breaking down in tears, so I remained there motionless, holding my breath.

"So? Lost your voice now, have you? Don't you try being clever with me. If I find out that all this is just because you don't feel like singing today, I promise you I'll make sure you'll never want to play at being a comedian again."

My father lifted his hand to run his fingers through his hair, but I was such a bundle of nerves that I thought he was about to hit me, and I lifted my arms to protect myself. Amjad thought this was so funny, he burst out laughing. That was when he received a loud smack across the head—it came from my mother, who'd just returned home from the shops and found this little scene being played out before her.

"What's going on here?"

My father turned suddenly—he wasn't expecting my mom to intervene, and certainly not in this way.

"What's going on is that Ahmad here says he can't sing any longer. But yesterday his voice was fine. He's making a fool out of me, that's what's happening."

"Wafik, how long has it been since you actually spoke with your son? I mean, apart from the singing lessons."

My father's eyes moved between me and my mother. "What do you mean? I speak with my son every day."

"Oh, yes? So how come you haven't noticed that his voice is breaking? He's fourteen; it's normal at his age. It's not his fault. He's growing up."

My father stood stock-still, his mouth open. Now he understood. He looked at me with his eyes full of sadness and disappointment, as though I were some kind of broken toy, completely useless to him.

He said nothing, but he picked up his jacket, which he'd thrown on the sofa, put on his shoes, and pulled open the bolt on the door. I closed my eyes, waiting to hear the sound of the door slamming, but there came no noise, no shouting, nothing.

When I opened my eyes again, my brother had gone. The room was empty except for my mother, who was standing on the threshold of the living room. She came over, leaned toward me, and hugged me. Only then did I burst into tears. I cried for hours, incessantly, while she held me in her arms.

I WAS IN MY ROOM, on my own, looking out of the window as usual. My elbows were resting on the windowsill; my eyes were lost in the blue sky. This had become my favorite pastime.

Suddenly, a little dot appeared among the clouds and started moving gently toward me. Here it was, finally. I'd been waiting for it. It was a spirit; it was *my* spirit, in a form of a tiny fairy with a glowing halo and wide, golden wings. As it descended, its velocity increased until it plunged straight into the center of my chest. The impact made me jump. I felt it enter me and rush through every corner of my body: the sweetest shiver ran through my veins, my bones, under my skin. Then it reached my back—I felt the pressure under my shoulder blades. The muscles tensed and my shoulders stretched farther apart. The sensation was painful, but at the same time it was also liberating. Finally, my skin gave way and opened, releasing the two majestic wings with their long, pointed feathers from my body—wings just like those of the black kites, the birds of prey I would often watch flying over the desert.

And so the magic began. My clothes tore, and the wings lifted me from the ground and allowed me to float between the walls of the room. My body cut through the air—light, as though weightless now, and moving freely, in harmony with my soul. My legs were springs that had launched me into flight; my arms were long, extended, and the tips of my fingers could brush the sky. This was my peace, my redemption—the only moment in which I could escape from a reality that suffocated me more and more, forcing me into a life of imprisonment and solitude. It was my biggest secret.

At a certain point, I felt the full weight of my body pinned to the floor. Suddenly, just as it had arrived, my spirit disappeared. But why right now? Perhaps something had upset it? Instinctively, I turned my head toward the door, and in the crack of light where it was slightly open (my grandmother and her mania for never letting the doors be properly closed), I made out my father's silhouette. It was there just for an instant, and then disappeared. I heard his heavy footsteps move away and go up the stairs to his apartment, two floors above.

Fear gripped me. I was alone, sweating, almost naked in the middle of the room. A terrible sense of fear took my breath away—I knew I'd been doing something that wasn't allowed. Something wrong was happening. "Why him?" I thought to myself, with my head in my hands. Of all people who might have seen me through the crack in the door, it was my father who had violated my intimacy. And now? What would happen now? Threats, sanctions, violence . . . what was in store for me? I had to find out, immediately. That way, I'd have more time to get ready for the worst. I put on the first pieces of clothing that came to hand and followed him, on tiptoe, up the stairs.

I opened the door delicately and fumbled my way along the dark corridor of my parents' apartment. I could hear their voices coming from the kitchen—they were keeping their voices down because it was late and my brother and sister were probably already asleep. I got as close as I could, my back against the wall and my ears tuned—I was only a few feet away from them.

"I no longer understand him. I almost feel now as though I don't know him," my father said.

"But you have never known him."

"Are you kidding? What do you mean I've never known him? He's my son. It's just that . . . recently he no longer seems to be himself. It's as though he's living in another world."

"So why don't you try to speak to him. Build some sort of relationship with him?"

"But I've always done that! We've done many things together—the music, painting . . . "

"Forget about music and painting. Those were things you wanted to do, not him."

"Listen, I've never forced my son to do anything, never. I just gave him the opportunity. If he wasn't interested, he could have told me."

"Wafik, that's not how these things work. When you ask the child if he wants to do something, he'll never respond sincerely. It's not because he's a liar, but simply because he doesn't know—he's still too young to decide these things for himself. Maybe he says yes because he's afraid of how you'll react, not because he really wants to do what you suggest."

In the silence that followed, I could hear my father's fingers drumming on the table—he always did that when he was upset. Then he cleared his throat and spoke again. "And what about this dancing in his room? Almost naked! Explain that to me, since you know him so well."

"I never said I know him that well; I said that you don't know him well enough. And I see nothing strange in the fact that he dances—ever since he stopped singing, he's lost a part of himself, he no longer knows who he is. That's why he's become so introverted. He is going through a bad time. You have to show a little patience; he's looking for himself."

"And he's looking for himself by dancing like a woman? Let's hope he finds himself soon because I will have no effeminate male in my house."

"See what you're doing? How can you ever build up a relationship with your son if you have all these prejudices in your head? Anyway, today I spoke with the psychologist from the school, and do you know what she said? 'Let him do what he wants to do.'"

"Ah! So you already knew that he was dancing?"

"Of course I knew. I told you—you don't know your own son."

"Couldn't you have told me, instead of going to see the psychologist? Would that have been such a bad thing?"

"Come on, Wafik, you must know how many times I've tried to talk to you, and you always tell me to keep quiet because you're watching television. And that's when you're at home. Usually you're out enjoying yourself, who knows where."

"Who knows where? At work, that's where. Breaking my back for all of you. If I didn't bring the money home, then what would you all eat? Explain that to me."

I'd heard enough. I went back down the corridor and closed the door behind me without worrying about making noise—my parents were now shouting so much that they'd never notice. I went back to my room and went to bed.

What my mother had said was true. Ever since I'd stopped singing, I no longer existed for my father. I'd become invisible to him. And I liked that, because it made me feel free. So why, at that moment, would I have given anything to have him come to me to talk, perhaps even to shout at me, but just to try to create some sort of dialogue, some sort of contact?

I turned on my side, gazing through the window, searching for my spirit lost somewhere in the starry sky. Perhaps instead of my father, my spirit would return to me. And this time I'd use its wings to fly away, far from everything and from everyone. But it didn't happen; from that day, it would be years before my spirit reappeared. I closed my eyes, but sleep wouldn't come. All around me were the silence of the night and the noise of my thoughts.

LOSING MY SPIRIT made me feel very lonely. I tried to call it back many times by dancing. But it never appeared, as if it were scared to return to that room.

Out of sorrow, I even left my friends and no longer played with my cousins. At school, I kept to myself. One of the teachers, a beautiful and warm woman, noticed the change and asked to talk with me. She asked me why I was lonely and why I didn't have friends. I told her about the spirit. She told me that she wanted to talk to my mother.

My mother met with my teacher. After the meeting, my mother told me that she had explained about my dancing. She also said that my teacher advised her to send me to the main dance company in Damascus, Enana Dance Theater, which had been founded by Jehad Mufleh in 1990 in Al-Yarmouk, where he was born. The company eventually moved to the main theater, just beside the Opera House in the Damascus city center, where it held most of its shows and from where it toured internationally. I was very excited to hear of my teacher's advice, but I knew it had to be a secret. My mother and I agreed that I should participate in the next audition. She promised to support me if I were accepted after the audition, and we agreed that we should keep it all as our secret.

Finally, I saw on television that the theater had announced an audition for new dancers. I couldn't wait for my mother to come with me, so I went to the audition alone. I was really nervous. The line of people—so many different types of people—filling in applications was long. Although I felt insecure, I said to myself, "I'm not leaving here before I try."

I went inside the dance studio, where there was a table full of judges and two dancers, young women, who were there to show the movements to the applicants. Along with two other applicants, I was to follow the movements of these two dancers. But my attention was caught by a beautiful blond woman who looked at me with big blue eyes. She was very different from anyone I'd ever seen before. Her shining eyes seemed to tell me that she was free and strong and full of energy, like my mother. I felt a beautiful connection with her. After I did the exercises and the movements, the judges asked me to go to the office, where they told me that I was accepted! I walked home in a cloud of happiness. I couldn't wait to tell my mother, who hugged me and said, "You just found your path, and you will shine through it if you are strong enough."

A month later, the company telephoned with the date of the first ballet lesson. Time crawled. When I entered the theater for the first class, I felt the theater's history and energy, as if the spirit of all the artists who had performed there remained. I could feel their energy, their spirit, and their dreams.

In that first ballet class, I retreated to the corner, as I was so shy and insecure. Then the blond woman entered the studio like a proud queen walking toward her throne. She looked at me with the same wide, shining blue eyes, but this time with a little smile.

She asked me to stand in the center of the dancers and asked them to wear the same type of training clothes that I was wearing. So everybody looked at me, which made me feel small and uncomfortable. I wished they would look away as soon as possible. Then suddenly, we heard the woman introduce herself as Albina Belova. She was our ballet master. She turned the music on and started teaching us.

The way that she commented and corrected us, and her care and energy, made me feel as if I were receiving special attention from her. She took care of me. It was as if she were teaching only me. I loved hearing her call my name, "Ahmad," in her Russian accent. Also, she was teaching during her pregnancy, but as she approached her final month she couldn't dance anymore. Sitting in her chair, she would verbally explain the exercise, and it was my responsibility to show the movements to the rest of the class. I would show up at the dance studio two hours before the start, and I was the last to leave. On my way home, I would review the class in my mind. As soon as I arrived home, I would go to my room and rehearse the lesson with the door locked.

Within a year, I was performing with the company. My first show was at the Roman Theater in Palmyra, where my mother was originally from. Without telling my father, she came to see me dance in the show, where she and Albina met for the first time. It was such a special experience to have these two strong mothers watch my first stage performance. I gave everything I had to that show. My spirit was there with me.

BUT IT WAS A DIFFERENT STORY with my father. Since the night when he and my mother talked after he saw me dancing in my room, his attitude changed. He really did try to be more present, to spend time with me even when there was no particular reason for him to do so. He tried to be a father and to treat me like a son. The atmosphere between us was generally pleasant, but deep inside I still felt a constant tension that kept me on edge, because of my secret: I was a member of Enana Dance Theater, where I had been for a year.

By this time, I was seventeen. My father knew nothing of my real life. He didn't know why, on returning from school, I would eat lunch in a rush and then go out again immediately. He didn't know that rather than meeting up with my friends and doing my homework with them, I was running off to practice classic ballet. He might have suspected something, but he never asked me about it. Parents often do that—they avoid asking questions so as not to receive answers they won't like.

My mother kept the secret, as we had agreed, for she was sure that if my father found out, my career as a dancer would be over at once. Unbeknownst to him, she gave me all the support she could—she lent me her tights for the classes and her makeup for the shows. I knew I could count on her completely, and this gave me the strength to keep going.

And so, constantly looking over my shoulder and being careful not to leave any evidence behind me, like a killer or a secret agent, I sought to fulfill my dream. There were the lessons, the shows, the constant struggle to juggle attendance at two schools, one of which was clandestine. But dancing filled me with joy, not just because of the activity itself, but because of the satisfaction of spending half of each day in an environment where I was accepted for what I really was, without having to pretend all the time. The secrecy was a strain, especially now that my father in some way was trying to reach a reconciliation with me. And yet I had no alternative—I wanted to dance.

But destiny had decided differently, and all my plans, which I thought were so well designed, fell apart in a matter of seconds. It happened in such a stupid way that even today I can't really come to terms with it.

One night, after I'd had dinner with my parents instead of my usual meal with my grandmother, my father sat on the sofa in front of the television and asked me to join him to watch a movie. The news was on, and the usual images of destruction and bombing, images we were now inured to. The news meant nothing to me: I wasn't interested in politics, and war for me was still an abstract and distant concept. But when that segment was over, the screen was suddenly filled with a familiar building—the very theater where my dance school was located. It was a news item about my school! They were showing everything: the theater, the rehearsal rooms, the outside walls of the building. My guts churned with fear—seeing my father watching my secret dance company on television was unbearable. What if I should appear?

I had to distract him. "Dad, why did this bombing happen?"

Surprised I should ask, he said, "They were attacking what they thought was a nuclear reactor."

On television, a journalist started speaking, talking about my dance company and its history, showing images and films from years back. This made me feel better; if it was just an item about the history of the theater, I had nothing to worry about. But to be on the safe side, I tried to keep his attention.

"And was there really a nuclear reactor there?"

"How would I know? One side says there was, the other side says there wasn't. Just let me watch this, please."

Perhaps he really was interested, even simply to show me that he was interested in dance; in any case, there was no distracting him from the television. The journalist stopped talking, and some music began, music I was horrified to recognize immediately, just as I recognized the images that went along with it: a clip from the show we'd done the week before in Palmyra. There we were, all made up and in costume, jumping around the stage, twirling away. It was a bright and cheerful scene, but my father was watching it with a weird look. He hadn't spotted me, but I was there . . . right before his eyes. My mother appeared in the clip, sitting in the audience, wearing a red shirt that made her easy to spot. Still my father didn't notice.

I panicked and jumped to my feet—I had to do something to avoid being found out. I stood in front of the screen and, putting as much enthusiasm as possible into my voice, said: "It's been ages. What do you think about the idea of me singing again? I think I could manage it now." I would have done anything to avoid the disaster that was beginning to seem inevitable.

My father looked at me in astonishment. He couldn't fathom my behavior and didn't know what to say to me. Perhaps it was because he wanted to think about it, perhaps it was just to shut me up for a moment, but all he said to me was, "Go get me a glass of water."

I had no choice but to obey, or else I would have increased his suspicions, and who knows what would have happened. But just as I started moving, I saw him jump. He then uttered a little cry—half fear, half incredulity—and I turned toward the television and . . . there I was: a detailed close-up of my face, in full makeup, covering the entire screen. My father was looking at it as though he'd seen a monster or a ghost, some horrible, repugnant creature. But it was me, his son.

He turned to me like a wounded beast, his face contorted with anger and pain. He started shouting, the veins in his neck and his forehead engorged and pulsing. Random words to begin with, not really sentences. Then all his rancor took shape in a series of accusations that fell on me like blows from a whip. He told me I was an ingrate, heartless. He threw in my face every effort and sacrifice he had made for me since I was born, and all his expectations for me that I had destroyed. He shouted that I was no longer his son—I was his shame. Even when my mother heard the shouts and came from the kitchen, it was impossible to calm him down.

That evening was the beginning of the end. My secret dancing was over; if I wanted to continue with my passion, I would have to do it openly, in a daily challenge to my father and his will. And he would try in every way possible to make me change my mind, by persuasion or by force.

And it was even worse than that: our family was now split into two clear and irreconcilable factions, with my mother and me virtually alone against all the others. Out of this fracture came the monster that had eaten away at me for years, the monster that had consumed and exhausted me, had made me ill both physically and mentally, had sent me over the edge in the worst moments, had crushed me when I was at my weakest.

Something died that evening, but something else was born. And while my father shouted, waving his arms frenetically in the air, throwing stuff around the room, my mother and I understood that from that moment, we would have to manage on our own. That was when, with a simple glance, we promised each other that we would always be there, the one for the other, despite everything.

TREE AFTER TREE. Building after building. The bus was moving quickly through a landscape that was becoming ever more familiar. Behind us was the desert, before us the outskirts of Damascus, gray and angular. I would have liked to stop time so that I never arrived there. Or, even better, to turn back and relive once again, even a hundred or a thousand more times, the emotions of the previous week. I was sure that everyone on the bus had the same thoughts—no one wanted to abandon that magic and inspirational atmosphere to return to daily life.

We'd been on tour with the dance company. We'd traveled for a week—a new town and theater every day, performing in various places throughout Syria. One show after another, with no hanging around—straight onto the bus to the next town. There was no room for tiredness, fear, or sadness, just an extraordinary energy that kept us going day after day, with big smiles on our faces and a profound sense of peace in our hearts. And yet, now that the tour was over, I suddenly felt exhausted. And worried.

The world of dance was a rich and all-consuming one that I would never grow tired of. But unfortunately, it wasn't my only world. There was another one that I had to live in, whether I liked it or not—my home life, which was completely different, made up of lies and subterfuge, of lowered gazes and silences, of feelings of guilt and frustration.

It was as if my heart were split in two, with me unable to give up either half. And being always on this edge affected not just me but my entire family. At the very moment when I put the permission form for participating in the tour, a form to be signed by an adult as I was still a minor, in Uncle Mahmoud's hands for him to sign, I knew perfectly well what was in store for me. My uncle and his wife, Areej, liked dancing, so I could consider them my accomplices. Aunt Areej used to prepare a box of food for me to take to the company. But Uncle Mahmoud was also my father's brother, and that meant running a big risk. If my father ever found out about the lie, then he and his brother would be enemies. But despite this, my uncle chose to sign the form.

My father—in the last analysis, like some inevitable verdict, it always came down to him. I'd managed not to think about my return home for the whole week, but now it was imminent, and I couldn't pretend nothing was wrong. I'd justified my absence by saying that I was going to Palmyra for a week to stay with my maternal grandparents. Had he believed me? Or had he been astute enough to uncover my lie? What lay in wait for me once I got home?

The youngest member of the company interrupted the flow of my thoughts. "I'm going out tonight," he said. "My folks want to celebrate my return. What about you?"

He had a slender and briskly powerful body that managed to jump higher than anyone else—a born soloist, with a bright mind and an endearing cheekiness that made any question he asked acceptable.

I fumbled for an answer. "Yes, of course. I'll be celebrating with my folks too. I can't wait."

When I got home, there was noise on the stairs, a confused coming and going that came from above, probably from the top floors. I walked up in silence, looking in at every landing to try and understand what was going on, and when I reached the fourth floor, which seemed to be empty, I wondered if maybe I should run back down rather than continue. But where could I have gone, alone and penniless? Putting the problem off wasn't going to help solve it. And then my home was there, on the fifth floor. For a little while, I'd been living in the apartment my grandfather had built for me. As I approached, I clearly heard movement inside. I took a deep breath and went up.

I hadn't even reached the landing when I saw my world come tumbling down. On the last flight of stairs, some cardboard boxes had been dumped, and in those that were open I saw my clothes, my books, and other belongings. Next to the boxes, lying on the stairs and leaning against the walls were the pieces of my dismantled bed and desk. I had been ejected from the apartment. Everything that represented my private life and independence lay there, in pieces, waiting for someone to come and take care of it, like junk left on the sidewalk.

I made my way through the boxes, my bag still over my shoulder, shocked and silent. The door to my apartment was open. At the end of the corridor, her back to me, was a woman, wearing pajamas. It was not my mother. She was busy removing things from a basket at her feet. I walked up to her without saying anything, incapable of speech. At a certain point, she must have realized I was there, because she finally turned and saw me.

"Welcome back, Ahmad," she said

"Who are you?" I replied.

"I am Wafik Joudeh's woman. I'm sorting out the apartment where we're going to live together. I've seen your photos. You look more handsome in real life. I heard you are a dancer. How cool!"

Her words were like a punch in the face. I didn't know how to react, what to think. I just stood there, motionless, staring at her. But my face was contorted; she was probably frightened now. I saw her step back slightly.

And then I came to myself. Moving slowly, I turned and picked up my bag, which had fallen from my shoulder and, without saying a word, went down the stairs and left the building. I felt as though I was about to faint, so I sat on the sidewalk. My hands were shaking, my head buzzing, the world around me spinning.

My father had a new woman. I had known that he and my mother were no longer getting on, but I'd never imagined things had reached this point. But this wasn't the worst of it. He had brought his new woman home, to *my* home. To the apartment I'd built with my grandfather. It was mine by right, and no one could take it away from me. Rather, that's what I'd always believed.

I ran my hand over my face and found it wet when I looked at it—I didn't know if it was sweat or tears. The street was empty. All I heard was an occasional voice from the open windows. I was alone and without a place in the world. I felt as though I might as well just stay there on the sidewalk, my dance bag at my feet, ready to be used the following day. I'd just sit there until the sun set on everything and the night made me, finally, invisible.

My family remained in the same building. The number of floors hadn't changed, the faded paintwork on the walls, the tiles, the furniture, nothing was any different. At first sight it was the same, but I felt that something profound had altered. It was as though the entire building that had been my home was now full of cracks.

My family was now held together by inertia; love no longer united it. Deprived of my apartment, I had to move down to live with my mother in the big family apartment. I picked up my things in silence and moved them into the family apartment. I reassembled my bed and desk and sorted out my clothes, finding space for them among my brother's stuff, even though we still weren't really getting on very well.

It was clear that for most members of my family, there was really only one problem—me, that I did not obey my father. It was my fault that my parents had separated, my fault that things had gone badly at home, my fault that our family had fallen apart. I felt this in the way they looked at me, in their silences, in the way they pretended not to see me whenever our paths crossed. I wished they would at least say something. I could have at least replied, explained myself, cleared a few things up. But nothing was said: their accusations were always lurking there in the shadows, ruining every minute of all my days.

After I returned from the tour, the first contact I had with my father took place on the stairs. I was going up and he was coming down. Suddenly we were face-to-face, forced into a contact that we'd both been avoiding for a month.

We looked straight into each other's eyes. But nothing happened. He said nothing, I said nothing. But even without words, I could hear his voice shouting in my head, saying that I'd deceived and wounded him, and that it was my fault that he'd become a neighborhood joke. In my head, he shouted that I disgusted him, that I was a worthless traitor, an egoist who thought only of myself; that I didn't love him; that I wasn't worthy of being a member of his family. With his eyebrows knitted, his fingers gripping the handrail, he looked at me and silently communicated all these things to me, until, under the weight of these intolerable accusations, I retired from the silent battle, moving out of the way to let him pass.

After that, his voice ringing relentlessly in my head, I went through my days as though carrying out some macabre ritual: I went to school every morning and dedicated my afternoons to lessons and rehearsals with the company. In the evening, I retired back into my shell to go home. This was a compromise I could accept only because every day, in the rooms at the dance school, I was able to finally let myself go. In there, I could jump, sweat, concentrate, dance—that was where I truly lived, freely expressing everything that I had to suppress whenever I opened the door to our building.

Dancing was the only safety valve I had. As I grew up, I became shyer and more solitary. What happened in my family was partly responsible for this, but I also struggled to establish relations with others and had very few friends. Real friends, I mean. The only person who was always stubbornly on my side was my mother. She, too, had her problems, but there was a tacit agreement between us never to talk about these things—we were always united and permanently on guard, she and I, alone against the entire building.

AFTER THAT BRIEF meeting on the stairs, I did everything to avoid my father. When I got home each evening, I'd creep up the stairs in the dark, feeling my way, being careful to make no noise. If anyone switched the light on, I'd move quickly to hide myself until the coast was clear. It was humiliating, of course, but it was better than finding myself face-to-face with him again. I didn't want to relive that humiliating experience, not for anything in the world.

But things were bound to come to a head with my father. One evening, I'd tiptoed up to the family apartment and, almost holding my breath, opened the door and slipped in. As I was about to close the door, I saw him, motionless, halfway down the corridor. "What is he doing here?" I thought. Can't he just stay upstairs, with his new woman? Why has he come down to torment us here in our home?" I became nervous.

He stared at me in the gloom of the corridor, and his face crumpled into a look of sheer disgust. His eyes became small and narrow. And nasty. He moved toward me quickly, as if in the throes of an uncontrollable instinct. Before I realized what was happening, he hit me in the face, hard, between my left eye and my nose. I wasn't ready for it and fell, blacking out for a few seconds before coming to and finding myself floored, my legs in the apartment, my upper body and aching head out on the landing. I tried to get up, but he punched me twice in the ribs. I stopped moving. I could see his bloodshot eyes, the veins in his neck standing out, his nostrils flared—an image I'd witnessed many times before, but never like this. There was something truly terrible in his gaze, an almost animal ferocity I hadn't come across before and which, more than the physical violence, kept me glued to the floor.

"How dare you come into this house in this way," he hissed.

He had seen me creeping up the stairs and was punishing me for my cowardice.

"Aren't you ashamed of going around like this after all the hurt you've caused us?"

"Me?" I said. "You're the one who's hurting everyone. What about *her*, the woman who's living up there in my apartment?"

Again he kicked me in the ribs. "Don't you ever dare, understand? And enough of this dancing business!"

I'd lost my head by this point. Rage, fear, and pain were burning me up. "No, Dad, you're the one who hasn't understood. Dancing is everything for me. Either I dance, or I die."

The words came out of their own accord, without me having to think about them. For anyone who didn't know me, these words might have sounded over the top, unreal, but for me it was pure truth, and I was ready to sign to it in blood. There was no compromising, no *more* compromising—if I couldn't dance, then I might as well die.

My father looked at me with his mouth open and his eyes full of hate. I waited for him to reply, but he said nothing. He grabbed my ankle and, with all his anger and all his might, he twisted it. Pain shot through my whole body, up my leg, through my guts, my back, my head. It was as though my brain were about to explode. I screamed. I'd never felt such pain in my life. I twisted on the floor while my father continued to press down on my ankle with his hands. He wasn't going to stop until he'd shattered my ankle—the look on his face left no doubt about that.

From behind him, two hands grabbed his shoulders and pulled him away from me. My mother. She shouted at him, insulted him, even tried to hit him and push him out of the house. But she couldn't—he was much stronger and completely crazy. He freed himself and elbowed her violently in the belly. She fell back onto the wall and slid to the floor, winded.

I tried to get up but couldn't—my ankle hurt too much. A sudden silence fell over the building, broken only by my mother's moans and my father's labored panting as he tried to get his breath back. He stood there in the middle of the corridor, between his son and his wife, both of us on the floor. Now he too was scared, you could see it in his face. He was shocked and terrified by what he'd done to two people who should have been among the most precious in his life. He put a hand on the wall to steady himself and then saw the open door, and in a flash he was out the apartment, running away.

The quiet was total now. And ominous, like the quiet after a violent storm. I grabbed the door frame with both hands and managed to pull myself off the floor. I hopped over to my mother and helped her get up. I pretended not to feel any pain and helped her over to the sofa, where she sat. I put a cushion behind her head and went to the kitchen to get some ice for both of us.

As I was getting the ice packs ready, my mother started sobbing and crying desperately, in a way I'd never heard her cry before. My physical pain was swept away by a more profound suffering, much more serious than a broken bone, heavier than a father's disappointment. This was the worst feeling I'd ever had in my life—I felt guilty for my mother's tears. She was the only person in the world who'd always supported me unconditionally, through everything. Her love for me had ruined her life, and now I was responsible for a further, terrible suffering. My mother, the last person who should have been hurt.

I was shattered. With my head leaning against the kitchen shelves, I started crying too. The more I cried, the more I wanted to cry, to free myself of all the hurt I'd caused and all the hurt I'd received, the pain that gripped my chest like a vise.

It took me ten minutes or so to get my breath back. My head was throbbing, with the same rhythm as my ankle. I touched my face, and my hand came away black and glittering. I moved to the mirror and saw that I still had my makeup on. I'd forgotten to remove it after the show. It had simply slipped my mind and I hadn't noticed. But my father had. That was what had driven him mad. He'd lost his mind because of my absentmindedness. So everyone else was right. It really was my fault.

Angry now, I rinsed my face and returned to the room. I wanted to apologize to my mother, throw myself at her feet, invent something to make her smile. But when I saw her, I stopped cold. She was no longer sobbing. Now she was lying on the sofa, pale as a sheet, her head twisted to one side. Her fingers were spread wide, placed either side of her belly. Her legs lay seemingly lifeless, her skirt raised halfway up her thighs. On the inside of her legs, two little rivers of dark red liquid ran down past her knees, her calves, her ankles.

I was paralyzed with terror. My mother was five months pregnant with a baby boy, and I had been so excited at the idea of having a new baby brother. But looking at her bloodied legs, I realized my father's violent blow to her belly had really hurt her—and hurt my new brother. I knew he was gone.

I threw myself on her and held her tight. I wanted to hold her in my arms and never leave her. Our tears started falling once more, flowing into a single, troubled river that perhaps, finally, would carry us away.

"Gently, Ahmad. You're hurting me," she whispered, her voice just a slender thread.

AFTER THAT TRAGIC incident with my father, my mother and I left home. We moved into an apartment that some friends of the family had kindly offered to us for a low rent. There were two mattresses donated by an acquaintance, and nothing else. We stayed there together, with our hearts full of sadness and fear. My mother was devastated by the loss of her baby, her home, and her husband, whom she'd always loved. She lost a lot of weight, but she continued going to work as if nothing had happened. During the day, she met people with smiles and kindness, but at night the tears came. She tried to hide them, but I saw everything. She taught me that the kindness can still glow, no matter how much pain one has in the heart.

But the conditions were terrible, and the stress intense. I had to care for my mother, who had lost a child. I had to maintain my dancing with the company. And I had to prepare for my final exams at high school. As the son of two teachers, it was very important that I pass these exams. But the day before the exams, I fainted during rehearsals with the dance company. After I was sent home, I started to feel intense pain in my stomach, which became stronger and stronger until I started vomiting blood. It was two in the morning. My mother was beside herself. In spite of the terrible things my father had done to her, she had to call him. She was afraid for my life. He arrived and drove me to the hospital. He and my mother fought verbally all the way there, with me in the back seat, crying with the pain.

I had an emergency appendectomy that day. But I had studied hard; I was ready for the exams. I convinced my father to help me slip out of the hospital the following morning so that I could take the exams. I refused to look him in the eye. Even though his help was the last thing I wanted, I had no choice. I had to wear a gallabia, a traditional Muslim robe, because with the fresh wound from the operation, I couldn't wear trousers. Walking was really painful.

Yet no sooner had I sat down at the exam desk than the stitches opened, and I had to go straight back to the hospital. This time, my mother was able to take me. I couldn't bear being with my father again.

Back in the lonely apartment I shared with my mother, lying on one of the skimpy mattresses, I felt like a complete loser. Even the walls shouted out just how miserable my existence was—a series of patches covering up wounds that continued to bleed, wounds that I knew I'd be carrying around for the rest of my life. Even dancing was no longer a consolation: some of my colleagues in the dance company were jealous of me because the choreographers were always giving me the best parts in the shows, and, being mean-spirited, these colleagues ostracized me and bad-mouthed me behind my back. Their behavior wounded me deeply; if my greatest passion, the one I'd willingly accepted a hellish family life for, was now against me, then what remained of my life?

The door opened suddenly. I could tell from the click of the door handle that it wasn't my mother, and even before I saw him,

I knew it was my father. Despite the fact that we'd left home, he would drop in to torment us. He had a knack of arriving at the worst moments. I dragged myself upright and sat on the mattress, because I didn't like having my back to him. Apart from this, I was so apathetic and lacking in energy that his presence brought no other reaction from me.

He started shouting at me. "I've just seen my brother, who told me you failed your exam. Congratulations—you're really building a great future for yourself."

He waited for me to speak, but I didn't open my mouth and I didn't move an inch. So he stirred things up even more.

"Maybe that school was too much for you. Maybe you should try something a bit more your level . . . maybe a kindergarten. Somewhere where they can toilet train you and teach you to speak like a man."

Still I didn't respond.

"Just look at you," he said, gazing around our apartment with a look of disgust. "But I guess you got what you deserve. I guess you and your mother like living like this."

There was contempt in his eyes and a spark of gratification that we'd been forced to live like this because we'd rebelled against him. If we'd kept quiet and been good, under his thumb, without ever lifting our heads, none of this would have happened.

"Don't think you're free of me just because we no longer live under the same roof," he added, as though reading my thoughts. "You need someone to teach you the hard way how life works, and that's what I'm here for. You should be thanking me for the patience I'm showing in still taking an interest."

My silence continued to irritate him. But I'd lost interest in everything—the room, my father, my school, even dancing. Anyone could have said or done anything without getting the slightest reaction from me. I just sat on the mattress with my back against the wall, my head tilted slightly to one side and my eyes staring into space.

"Come on," he said. "Say something. Do something."

I looked at him, making no move, for seconds that seemed like hours.

"Good. Whatever. If you're so keen to stay at home and sleep, go ahead. Maybe in the long run you'll get bored, and you might even want to study."

I didn't move as I watched him open the door, leave the apartment, and close the door behind him, but not before he'd given me one last stare and said, "I don't understand you, Ahmad."

I thought of my mother. She was the one who kept saying, "You have to accept it, you have to maintain relations because one day, you might want to go back to live in your real home and abandon this dump."

I knew that she was still cooking for my father every now and then, in spite of the horrible thing he had done to her, as though he'd never done her any harm. I was convinced that she and I no longer had anything in common with our family, if it could still be called that. But my mother still loved my father, and this difference led to arguments and bad feelings between us. It hurt me to fight with her—the two of us had no one in the world except each other.

I don't know how long I sat there, in that same position. Hours, probably, because in the window I could see that the light had faded and darkness filled the room. I thought of nothing; all I did was feel my body in all its heaviness. My legs were heavy, spread out on the mattress. My back heavy against the wall, my head so heavy it barely managed to stay upright. My arms were heavy, lying loose on my thighs. My fingers felt heavy, my nails, my eyelids, my skin, my muscles, my bones. Every bit of me seemed monstrously, unbearably heavy. I understood then that in order to feel better, all I had to do was to free myself of that weight, that burden.

I got up and went to the bathroom. I rooted through my few belongings, searching for the only object that could make me lighter. I found it. Without hesitating, I placed the razor blade on the inside of my left wrist and made a deep incision. I felt my weight evaporate, as if my body was levitating. The blood ran warm down my arm—it was leaving me and it made me free. But there still wasn't much of it. I put the blade to my wrist again and pushed with all my strength to make a second incision, even deeper this time. Only then did I lose consciousness, and at last I was flying.

FOUR

TWO LETTERS, ONE in each hand, both white envelopes, both of the same weight—a single sheet and a few drops of ink. I pulled them out and reread them for the twentieth time. I studied them carefully, front and back, waiting to see some detail spring out that canceled out their meaning—a name spelled incorrectly, a false date, or maybe even a message—"Just kidding!" But no, this time it was all real.

I carefully put the sheets back into the envelopes and closed them again. I hid one under my T-shirt, held by the waistline of my trousers, and kept the other in my hand. I went to my mother in the living room. We had returned to my apartment in the family's building following my suicide attempt. My father had sold the family apartment to buy a house for his new wife outside the family building and moved out of my apartment. My mother was on the sofa, leafing through a magazine.

"Ram, sorry for interrupting . . . there's something you should see." I said this with the most serious face in the world, trying hard not to burst into joyous laughter.

"Should I be worried?" she said, looking me a little anxiously.

"Mmm . . . perhaps yes, a bit."

She opened the envelope with a sigh—who knows what she was imagining. I saw her eyes cloud over when she saw that the letter was from my high school, and then they lit up with joy as she read through to the end.

"Ahmad Joudeh!" she shouted, jumping up to hug me. "You've done it, you've done it! You've finally passed the graduation exams!" She held me tight, as though I were still a little child, even though I had become much taller than she was. "Well, it took you three years, but with everything that's happened in the meantime . . . that's just fine, let's not think about it anymore. Now you're finally free!"

It was a year since my suicide attempt. I was now nineteen years old. I had become a soloist at the dance company and I was performing a lot, which helped me to overcome what had happened to my mother and me. My brother and sister were doing well in school too. Our success made our mother proud. She kept up her work as a teacher, and at home she made us feel like a family, even though our father was away. My father was still showing up from time to time. He knew how much my mother loved him, and how much I hated seeing him. I did my best to ignore him and listened to the inner voice telling me in my dreams that my future was worth fighting for, no matter what he said or thought about me.

"There's something else you should read," I said, pulling the second letter from under my T-shirt.

"Should I be worried again?"

"A bit more this time," I said with a smile.

She sat and read the second sheet of paper attentively. Then she read it again and looked at me with a quizzical expression. I sat down next to her—I owed her some explanations.

"This, Ram, is the response from the school I applied to. I didn't want to tell you anything beforehand because I didn't want you to be worried."

She continued to look at me in astonishment, lowering her eyes every now and then to the letter. It was obvious she wanted to ask me something, but she didn't know where to begin.

"It's the Higher Institute for Dramatic Arts in Damascus," I said. "They offer a course that lasts four years and covers everything about theater, from the history to technical things. And then there are the practical courses—all the subjects and a lot, a whole lot, of dancing. The school even has its own dance performances. I'm sorry I never mentioned it, but . . . I just wanted it to be something for me."

"And . . . it says here that they've accepted you, no? You'll be able to study there?"

"Yes, I can't believe it either, but it's true. I've done it."

"And are you happy?"

"Crazy happy!"

"In that case, I am too . . . and I'm very proud of you." As she said this, she pulled me toward her, and I ended up curled up on the sofa, my head on her legs. "You're a stubborn thing, aren't you? But if the things you do make you feel good, then that means it's the right choice."

"Thanks, Ram," was all I managed to say. And I thought the position she'd arranged me in was really uncomfortable, but I'd have liked to stay that way forever.

A few months later, on a beautiful September day with the sky free of clouds and a lovely breeze blowing, I was with my best friend, Saeed. After the torrid heat of the summer months, being outside was actually pleasant, and we were sitting on the terrace of the sports center café in the Al-Midan neighborhood of Damascus.

Saeed and I had been together at Enana Dance Theater for three years. He was specializing in hip-hop. At the sports center we were working together as coaches: Saeed was teaching break dancing, and I was in charge of the dancers' warm-ups. We were enjoying a few minutes of peace before returning to our homes, sitting where no one would bother us.

"Excuse me, coaches?"

Turning around, we saw a young guy standing there, gym bag over his shoulder and arms behind his back.

"I'm a student here at the center. I want to thank you for the class; it was really great. I like the fact that one of you deals with the warm-up," he said, looking at me, "and the other with the break dance," looking at Saeed. "You guys work so well together."

"Thanks," Saeed said. "Hope to see you at the next class then."

I could see that Saeed was politely trying to tell the guy that we wanted to be left alone. But he didn't leave. He stood there in silence, as though waiting for something.

"Yes?" Saeed asked.

"I was just wondering. Since you get on so well together, you work together, and you even look like each other . . . are you brothers?"

I spoke up. "No, we're not brothers, just friends. We met each other in a dance company. We got on great, and since then we've worked together."

"Oh. OK," the kid said, and walked off.

"What was that about?" I said. "A bit cheeky, yeah?"

"Well, he wants to be a dancer, right? And it helps to be a bit like that if you want to get ahead."

"A bit like what, sorry? Presumptuous?"

"Yes, sort of. A bit over the top. Get noticed, get heard. It's easier that way to be considered when they have to choose a dancer for a show."

I thought about this for a while. About how Saeed and I met. Our friendship. But also how different we were from each other. He was the type of person who wanted to get ahead, to be noticed. And like the kid we just met, Saeed knew how to draw attention to himself. But I hated that side of the business. For me dancing had never been a competitive thing, and he knew it.

"You know," I said, "the first time I saw you, I really didn't like you."

His eyes opened wide in surprise, and he looked at me directly, but without saying anything.

"Yes," I continued. "It was a birthday of someone in the dance company; it must have been three years ago. I was studying for my high school exams back then, so I hadn't been to classes and hadn't met the new arrivals. When I saw you in that bar, I thought you were just one of the birthday boy's friends and, really, instinctively I didn't like you at all."

Those three years felt like centuries to me. So many things had changed since then.

"But what had I done?" Saeed asked. I didn't know if he was more offended or curious.

"Nothing. You did a few break-dance moves. You were great, and the others were watching and trying to imitate you. It just seemed to me you were showing off, that's all."

"OK, but remember this? I came over to your table and introduced myself, and you paid no attention to me *at all*."

"Well by then, Saeed, you'd already made your mark. I couldn't help it."

We both laughed. The sun was setting, and it would soon be getting cold. But that moment was too precious for us to interrupt. Remembering our past conflicts reminded us of our present bond.

"When I came back to classes and rehearsals and saw you again," I said, "it was a shock, because I didn't imagine you'd be there. And that time you were even more in my face—you asked if I'd hurt myself because my wrist was bandaged."

"And you replied with a very elegant, 'Keep your nose out of it!'" he said, smiling.

We laughed again. Even that episode seemed light and distant, as though it belonged to another life. Life before meeting Saeed, the life I'd have to return to once we said good-bye.

"Do you know when I started liking you?" I said.

"No, but if you keep going like this, I'll get offended. I liked you immediately."

"Stupid. I started to like you when we were working with the company on the set of that film, that time when we were dancing for two months. I remember that every time I turned round, you were there, always close to me—it was as though you were doing it deliberately."

"Well, maybe I was. Who knows?"

"And then, one day, you appeared out of the blue and asked if anyone had ever told me that I had beautiful eyes."

"And you said yes, you'd already received that compliment. A regal response, Ahmad." His eyes were bright, and mine must have been too. The sun began to disappear behind the minaret.

"Let's go, what do you say?" he asked.

"Yes. It's getting chilly."

We set off walking homeward while the tired shadows of the buildings began to lengthen.

He said, "You know, having you beside me makes me feel so strong."

"I feel the same; you make me feel complete."

I looked into his eyes and said, "I promise, I will always be there for you."

"Me too, forever."

FIVE

AT FIRST, IT'S JUST *a slight trembling on the surface of the water in the glass that sits before you. A little rumble that gradually becomes stronger, and then you feel it inside—a shock that jolts your bones and shakes your blood. You know something is happening, but you don't know what it is. Then the whistling noise starts, first faint and then louder. It's followed by a long, deep thud that hits your guts. The glass in the windows starts trembling, as well as the plates, glasses, and saucepans in the kitchen—iron, ceramic, and glass play a military march, a long drum roll that announces the inevitable. It's clear now—they're on their way.*

This is the sound and feel of war. The sun has set and the shadows have dissipated into a black that covers everything. You'd like to go to sleep, but you can't, not now. The whistling sound is suddenly much louder, with no warning and no gradual increase—from faint and distant to penetrating and close. Then the thud, which this time is a great boom, a thunderclap in the storm, a landslide of rock down the mountain. A flash lights up the room as though it's daytime for a second or two—just long enough for you to see that the drawers have opened and your wardrobe doors are wide open, the clothes about to spill out, your books dancing on the edge of their shelves. You don't want them to fall. You rush to the light switch; the electricity's still there and you push everything back into place, but as you're doing this, you hear a great crash coming from the kitchen. You run there and find a cemetery of porcelain and glass shards covering the floor. Those were your plates and your glasses. You can't walk in the kitchen now. Another whistle, so strong you think it's entering one ear and exiting the other. The great roar this time has its epicenter between your eyes.

The shock wave strikes, and you think you're exploding—it travels quickly and envelops everything: lampshades fall, silverware jumps out of the drawers, cupboard doors spring open, and those that were open slam shut. The walls tremble and a white dust rains from the ceiling, followed by pieces of plaster as big as your face that shatter at your feet. The windows, too, explode, and glass splinters rain in all directions like projectiles—you can hear them flitting by your ears despite the infernal racket that surrounds you. Strips of the curtains flutter in the wind, and you watch the dust come in through the broken windows and torn fabric to settle on everything it meets. You cough, you can't breathe, you double up and put your hands on your knees—you don't know if it's you who's trembling or if it's the whole building.

You close your eyes and you hear it, the last whistling noise, the ultimate one. You know that after this, there will be silence and everything will finally stop shaking. So you wait. You concentrate on that sound and follow its trajectory until you become its body and you see with your eyes what it sees—beyond the pointed steel of its head, the smoking city is rushing closer. Looking carefully among the rooftops, you recognize your building, the only one still standing. You can see into it and you see yourself in there, your head tilted skyward and your arms wide open. You shout as loud as you can, so that the echo of your voice will be the only thing remaining when the silence comes. But the whistling sound is so much louder and it covers your voice completely. "You are no one," it tells you. You see the roof crack open; the metallic head penetrates the concrete as though it were butter, the walls crack under the stress and break into big blocks. Everything shakes. Everything collapses. The ceiling, the walls, the floors, you, your belongings, your life, your feelings. Everything is blended and becomes a single heap of rubble, indistinguishable from all the others.

"Ahmad! Ahmad, wake up!"

My hand was hurting because I'd been clenching it so tightly. When I loosened it, I realized it was holding something—another hand. I opened my eyes. It took a second or two for me to focus and then I recognized my mother, leaning over me. I was soaked with sweat.

"Sorry," I said. "I had a bad dream. You go to sleep; it must be late."

"It's actually only midnight. I was just about to go to bed."

I kissed her and thanked her. I turned on my side, hiding my head under the pillow. Midnight.

Not so good—I still had the whole night before me.

I HAD JUST TURNED twenty-two years old. The civil war in Syria that broke out the year before had been spreading more and more, like a cancer, eating the body of Syria and the mind of the people in it.

How did we get here?

It was difficult to say, especially for people like me who are not political, who are not even interested in politics. The first person to die in the Al-Midan neighborhood was a pupil of mine in my dance class—Shahid, which means "the martyr."

For me personally, the first effect of the war was a physical one—I began to suffer from terrible headaches, unpredictable and increasingly powerful, as though in some small way I was participating in other people's pain. I increasingly felt the urgent need to react, but I didn't want to shoot, to hurt anyone. I didn't want to add any more violence to the violence that was already there. So I made use of different "arms"—I opened up a basement school with Saeed not far from home, where I could teach dance, for a modest fee or for free for those who could not afford it, to the neighborhood kids, inviting anyone who might be interested. Saeed taught hip-hop, my sister taught gymnastics to groups of women in the mornings, and my mother looked after the logistics and made sure that everything was well organized—the courses, the timetables, the enrollments. As this was the first school of this kind in Al-Yarmouk, we were not sure if there would be any interest. To our surprise, however, the neighborhood reaction was excellent—those who came to us to dance could free their minds for a few hours every week.

I even started dramatizing the war, transforming horror into art, creating choreography for shows on the suffering that people lived through around me, trying to make those who were ignorant understand the level of horror with which we were living every day. For one show, I had the dancers take loaves dirtied with blood onto the stage, a detail that seemed to make a big impression on the audience, but it was nothing more than something I'd actually seen a few days before. When the audience left the theater, I saw people deep in thought, their eyes lowered and preoccupied, which was exactly what I'd been aiming at.

Another real result of the war was prices, especially the price of houses. The fighting had begun in the south, and great masses of people fled northward; as they moved up to Damascus, the cost of renting a house or apartment skyrocketed. Insult to injury. I'd heard a rumor that this was why my father was thinking of selling my apartment.

My father. I had never forgiven him for how he treated me and my mother, but the war was so overwhelming that the history between us, and everything to do with my family in general, had become of secondary importance. The chaos of the war, though it hadn't directly hit us yet, was creeping into every part of our lives. The few certainties we had were collapsing day after day, without leaving us any time to get used to it and reorganize ourselves. We felt that we were inexorably losing all values; we were becoming simply numbers, divided between those who were still alive and those who were already dead. And still nothing tangible had actually happened to us.

But I was dancing and doing better all the time. I had been given the role of lead dancer, the protagonist of the show, and this day in June I was heading to the Opera House in Damascus. I had agreed with Saeed that I should fetch him at his house in the Al-Midan neighborhood on the way.

I hadn't taken my bicycle that day because the latest skirmishes meant that the roads were blocked. Saeed's bike was broken anyway, and our plan was to travel together on public transport, if possible, as far as the Opera House. The farther I went from Al-Yarmouk and the deeper I went into Al-Midan, the more nervous I became about the dress rehearsals that I'd be doing in a few hours. As the lead dancer, I was responsible for the show's success or failure.

I knew my part well, but I couldn't help getting worked up. I also knew, however, that it was a good thing that I was feeling that way because going onto the stage without being scared could only lead to a poor performance. And yet I had to calm down, because this was "only" a dress rehearsal. The real obstacle to overcome was the night and day following the dress rehearsal, waiting for the premiere.

I went to Saeed's house—he'd know how to calm me down. I buzzed the entry phone, my bag on my shoulder. I was already impatient, eager to move again because I couldn't bear waiting of any kind.

"Saeed, it's me—come down now."

"But it's really early. What are you doing here already?"

"Just a bit early. That way, we won't be late."

"But I didn't expect you for another hour. Listen, I'm not ready yet. Come on up and have a cup of tea while I get dressed."

He buzzed me up and I went up the stairs, knocked on his door, and went straight through to the kitchen, where I said hello to his mother, who was already busy preparing my tea. Saeed's mother and I had known each other ever since I met Saeed.

"So, Ahmad, are you a bit nervous?" she asked, and went on to add, "Have you eaten well?" as she always did.

"Yes, I've eaten, thank you. But, well, Auntie, it's the first time for me to be lead dancer in a show in the Opera House."

"And what does that mean?"

"It means that I have to do the pas de deux with the lead ballerina. I'm on stage more or less all the time. It's. . . well, it's a big responsibility."

"That's wonderful. Don't you worry—you're good, I'm sure you'll do very well, Inshallah. The show's tomorrow, isn't it?"

"Yes. Will you come to see us?"

"Of course I'll come, I wouldn't miss it for anything in the world. Even if the world came to an end. Will your mother be there too?"

"I think she will."

She handed me a cup of tea, which despite the torrid summer heat I drank with gusto, and then I placed the cup on the table.

Then, I noticed what looked like ripples on the surface of the liquid. They were almost imperceptible, but there was something there. They disappeared immediately and then came back again. "Is it a hallucination? Another migraine? I really don't need this now," I said to myself (I had a medical history of migraines).

Then we heard it, and immediately we knew what it was, even though we didn't want to admit it. It was a low, deep sound, followed by the tinkling of the glasses on the shelves as they vibrated one against another. Auntie and I looked into each other's eyes without saying anything, just waiting for it to arrive. We heard a roar, like an old motorbike, but the closer it got, the clearer it was that this was no motorbike. It flew directly over our heads, and even Saeed, in the shower, must have heard it because he appeared in the kitchen after a few seconds, wearing his bathrobe and with his eyes wide open in a mixture of incomprehension and terror. We all knew what it was.

A sudden boom, and a shock wave that made everything shake, even the brains in our heads. The lampshade swung dangerously, the glasses fell from the shelves and shattered together with the teapot, which emptied its hot contents all over the floor. We looked at one another without moving—a building in the neighborhood had just collapsed after being hit by a bomb, and it could have happened to us. Another roar announced the arrival of another plane, bringing other bombs. We heard the machine-gun response of the antiaircraft guns through the general racket: the noise of the planes, the collapsing walls, the people shouting in the street.

Then we reacted. Saeed got dressed in the first clothes he could find, and without saying anything we rushed downstairs with his mother toward the shelter, which was the basement of the building. We kept our heads down without looking, without thinking, without even breathing. We rushed down the dark stairs that led to the shelter.

The basement shelter consisted of two rooms that had been used as a warehouse, and the available space was limited. It filled up quickly, especially with women. They had come down in the rush using whatever piece of fabric they could grab as their hijab. There were some who had not even had time to do that. To be respectful, Saeed and I stood apart from them, near the door. From there, we could hear everything—the cries of desperation, the sobbing of those who were wandering the streets in panic, the orders barked by fighters who were trying to take control of the situation but whose voices were full of the same terror we were feeling. And the shooting: hundreds of bullets and bombs—from the land, from the air, perhaps even some mortar shells from far off, the bombs landing, the concrete collapsing, the cars accelerating, braking suddenly, the machine guns, the sound of rifles and pistols. The women behind us crying and praying, holding their children to their breasts.

But I was thinking of just one thing—the dress rehearsal. I must have looked at Saeed in some particular way, or perhaps he just knew me too well, because out of nowhere, he said to me, in a soft but determined voice:

"Don't even think about it."

Fortunately I paid heed. I pulled out my cell phone and called the choreographer and the director to let them know that I couldn't make it. I spoke to my mother—she too was in a shelter and was fine. Then I received a message from my father, but I didn't reply—if he was really interested in how I was, he could call me. At that point, I resigned myself; we sat on the chilly stone floor and waited, because there was nothing else to do. The fighting seemed to be endless, and to go out would have been suicide. We discussed who might be fighting out there, but there was no way of knowing. All we could do was wait, and that's what we did.

I had the first twinge of a migraine, at the worst possible moment to have one. I knew that if I managed to sleep a little, then I could keep it under control, so I closed my eyes and concentrated on positive memories: my grandfather's face; my grandmother's hands; the roof of our house; and the spirit that accompanied me in my secret, solitary dancing, until I slipped into a restless sleep, under the constant sounds of bombs. With each bomb a person, or maybe an entire family, died; with each bomb a home collapsed, memories and histories disappeared underneath the rubble. How cruel could humans be to cause such a horror?

When we awoke the following morning, the situation seemed to be calmer. There was still some fighting, some shooting and shouting, but there were no aircraft or buildings collapsing. I looked around the shelter, and everything was just as it had been the night before—the women, some in their hijab, some with their long hair loose, held their children in their arms, in the same positions they had been in before I fell asleep. I wondered if they had slept. It was probable their husbands were out there. No one knew if they'd ever see them again.

I was still in contact with my family, and I knew that they were all well. This fact left some space in my head to think about something else—the show. If an entire night had passed, then that meant the premiere was that very evening. I had to get out of the shelter, I had to get to the theater, and the silence between one shot and another felt like an invitation to break free. I knew it was dangerous, but the force that was pushing me was the same that leads a man to pick up a rifle and risk his life. But those who fight are considered heroes, while I'm considered a madman.

I got up and took hold of the door handle. "Ahmad, what are you doing?"

It was Saeed's mother—terror in her voice.

"You can't go out, you can't. Saeed, you tell him. It's madness to go out there."

Saeed looked at us but remained silent. He knew that he wouldn't be able to make me see sense as he had done the night before, yet at the same time, he couldn't disobey his mother, whose opinion was certainly the most sensible.

"Auntie, with all due respect, up until now we've been lucky—no one's come down here and the building hasn't collapsed on top of us, but if anything does happen, then we'll be like mice in a trap. I don't want to end up that way—I prefer to die out there in the open, and in the light of day."

She didn't reply. She knew that I wasn't completely wrong, but at the same time she wasn't brave enough to make a move. I simply couldn't remain one second longer in that hole. I looked at Saeed, he nodded to me, and I opened the door and went out.

The fresh air in the stairway immediately filled my lungs and confirmed for me that being out there was the more bearable of the two options. It may have been more dangerous, but it was certainly better. I aimed to reach the theater, at any cost.

"What are you doing here?"

I'd reached the ground floor when I found a rifle pointed at me by a fighter with a surprised look on his face. He couldn't figure out where I'd appeared from, because together with other fighters stationed at the entrance and on the lateral windows, he'd already checked all the apartments on the upper floors and thought there was no one left in the building.

I thought I recognized the fighter; I'd already seen him somewhere, and his accent was from Al-Midan.

"What are you doing here?" I said.

"We're here to protect people like you."

This conversation was typical of the time: two men meeting who didn't know each other, being careful not to reveal too much, as they didn't know whose side the other was on. But I had understood immediately whose side they were on, and I was able to use this information, knowing their beliefs and their customs.

"If you really want to protect us, then you have to help us survive. All the inhabitants of this building are downstairs, in the cellar," I said, pointing to the dark corner and the stairway that he must have missed in his search. "It's full of women and children down there—you have to get them out and away from here as soon as possible."

The man looked where my finger was pointing and said nothing. He must have been surprised and ashamed to have neglected such an important detail. He turned his back on me—it was now difficult for him to take the upper hand—and he started talking in a low voice with his fighters. He returned after a few minutes.

"OK, you have to arrange a truck to get you out of here, and we will give you a sign when the fight is calming down."

Luckily, my phone was still working. I called my friend Mohammad, who had a truck. I asked him to come to rescue us; otherwise we would all die. Mohammad came very quickly with his big truck, risking his life.

"Mohammad, how could you pass the checkpoints?"

"I told them that I need to rescue my wife and kids."

"Thank you; I will never forget what you have done for me."

The fighter gave a sign to us, so I went back down and opened the cellar door, met now by stifled cries of terror.

"Don't worry, it's me again. We all have to leave. My friend is here with a big truck, and the fighters will help clear the way for us to escape. Bring the bare minimum; bring nothing at all if you can manage. We have to go up now and try to get on the truck. Everyone, upstairs and away from here!"

Apart from Saeed and myself, the only people left in the building were women, the elderly, and children. I realized this as I watched them file past me one by one, without protesting, completely overwhelmed by events and ready to obey any order that offered them the sensation of heading for safety.

We took up a position just behind the door, each of us with a child in our arms, ready to flee. I did a head count—there were about fifteen of us.

"Quick! Out of here and onto the truck without looking back! Are you ready? May Allah be with you."

As soon as the fighter opened the door, we were struck by the blinding light reflected from the sand. After all those hours in the dark, we couldn't see anything. But there was no time to get used to it, and with our eyes half-closed and watering, we pushed forward, toward the truck. The back gate was down. Saeed and I helped the others get in, and then we stood on the little back step of the truck trying to cover the kids so they would not be able to see what we were afraid they might otherwise see. When we were all aboard, I gave a sign to Mohammad, and he set off, foot to the floor.

I gradually got used to the light and began to understand what sort of truck this was—it was completely open. We were an easy target, and Mohammad drove zigzag at a crazy speed, while all around us we could hear the whistling of bullets that were probably aimed at us. The children were all at the center of the truck bed, with the women around them, and then, on the outside, Saeed and I and the older people. I could see it all clearly now, though the scene before me was one I'd have preferred not to witness: the hot sand on the ground was rippling with the waves of bullets hitting it, while Saeed and I were competing to cover each other. The wind spread the dust so that the entire neighborhood was immersed in a fine yellow mist. The walls of the houses were peppered with bullet holes, some small, some large, and from these holes cracks departed in every direction. Some houses no longer existed; in their places were unnatural, empty spaces, or at most the skeleton of a structure that somehow still managed to stand upright.

There were pieces, fragments, shards, rubble everywhere: unrecognizable objects that had broken loose and now lay on the ground. I looked closer. In the midst of the sheets of metal, the rusty iron pipes, and the legs of wooden chairs, I finally understood what these unrecognizable pieces were—bit of bodies, pieces of bodies spread all over the roads: hands, arms, strips of flesh whose origin was difficult to identify, protruding bones and lacerated and burned skin. The rest of the bodies must have been taken away. I was horrified; it made me feel sick. I tried to make sure that the children saw nothing of all this.

A car overtook us, and for a moment it was alongside us in front of me—a small city car with one man at the steering wheel. He had his foot down on the accelerator, and as we moved forward, the two vehicles swayed closer and moved away alternately. The driver's eyes were wide open; his hands gripped the wheel firmly, his body leaning forward. He too was running away. It seemed to me as though hours went by, but it was probably just a few seconds—he turned his head and saw me, we looked straight into each other's eyes. Right then, his windshield shattered, and at the level of his neck, a big piece of his skull came away as his brain exploded and his body was driven backward and his eyes rolled toward the sky. His car slowed down, but it didn't stop, it continued moving, curving slightly to the right. I couldn't take my eyes off it, following it until it was behind us, and from there I could see clearly the man's head tilted backward and the hole in his neck. This was a sniper's handiwork, probably the same sniper who'd been having fun with us.

We all made it. Mohammad got us out of the combat zone. As he returned to his work, I waved to him. Then I headed automatically for the theater, with Saeed following me in silence. We didn't utter a word the whole way, and we said nothing to the choreographer, to the director, to our colleagues. We danced, because that's what we were there for. During our final bow, I broke down in tears.

We spent that night in a hotel on Mount Qasioun, from which we had a view of the entire city. But Damascus was darker than usual that night; the only light came from the mortars that crossed the sky like shooting stars. The following day, having heard that the fighting had died down, Saeed and I returned to Al-Yarmouk. On arrival, I found Saeed's mother waiting for us at the door, her eyes swollen from crying. She looked at me and said, "An hour after you got us out of there, the planes came back. They bombed the building next to ours, so if we hadn't left . . . "

She started sobbing. We'd got away by the skin of our teeth. If it hadn't been for the premiere of our show, I'd still be down there. Saeed, his mother, all those women with their children, and me. Dance or die, I said to myself in my mind. Dance or die.

~

"AND TWO AND THREE and four and one and two . . . no, keep that leg up . . . and four, go ahead, breathe, shoulders down, elbows up."

I was conducting a dance lesson for the local kids in our basement school, as usual.

The hour of classical barre lesson was always torture for my students, but it was good for them—it straightened their backs, made them taller and more elegant. I think they themselves realized this because they came back every time; they must really have liked it.

"Teacher, can we take a break, please?"

"Teacher, I need the bathroom."

"I need to drink."

"All right, all right. Calm down. Five minutes to do whatever you like. But don't drink too much because your muscles fill with water and you'll have trouble lifting your legs."

It took just a few seconds for those perfect dancers to return to being the children they were—shouting, pushing one another, laughing. It was pointless telling them to keep quiet, so why bother? The school was one of the few safe places where they could be themselves, sheltered from the fighting between the rebels and the army, which was becoming more frequent as the conflict moved northward. It would be only a matter of a few months, or maybe weeks, before Al-Yarmouk would take center stage in the theater of war that played out every day on television.

In the midst of the general racket, I managed to make out the sound of the bell on the ground floor, which meant that the door had opened and someone had come in. As we were on break, I decided to go see who it was.

"Please, kids, I'm just going upstairs for a moment. Try not to create too much damage while I'm gone."

I went up the stairs and found my mother there. She was crouched on the floor, her face in her hands, crying as I'd never heard her cry before, crying so hard she had trouble breathing. I rushed to her and took her hands, uncovering her swollen, blood-shot eyes.

"Ram, what's happened?"

In the midst of her sobbing she had trouble speaking, and I made out just a few words. "At home . . . thrown out . . . his wife . . . selling the apartment."

I knew at once what she was trying to tell me. Three years ago, my father had sold the family apartment out from under us. Now he was selling mine. He had already said he would, even though my mother and I were living there, to take advantage of rising prices. His new wife must have been involved in all this, and it looked like they had thrown out my mother and me. I was wild with anger. I hadn't had any violent episodes with my father since the abuse that led to my suicide attempt, but our unresolved conflict was still in the air, and I hadn't forgotten anything of what my mother and I had been subjected to. All the contempt that I'd struggled to suppress returned to the surface, and I decided the moment had come for me to act. He had no right to treat us like this.

"Ram, I'm going to talk to him. The children are downstairs. You stay here with them, give them something to do, but don't move from here. I'll be back."

I left as my mother tried again to say something to me, probably telling me not to bother. But I wouldn't have listened to her, or to anyone else. Anger had made me blind and deaf. How dare he put the apartment up for sale? It was mine—my name was on the deed. He had lived there with his wife only because I let him, in order to avoid conflict. But he would never stop imposing his will on others, especially on me, as though avenging himself for the wrong he felt I had done him.

I ran the five blocks from our basement school to home in a few minutes and rushed up the stairs. Immediately, I heard loud voices coming from the first floor, from my grandmother's apartment. When I entered, I found them all there—some of my aunts and uncles, my grandmother, my father, and his wife, whom I couldn't bear seeing in the apartment of my childhood and adolescence.

"What are you doing here?" I asked her. "And who has thrown my mother out of her house?"

"It is not her house," my father said.

"Of course it is; the house of her children is also her house."

We continued in this vein for a few minutes, until his wife tried to intervene, and I grew so angry that I called her a word I would not want to repeat. It was the first time I had ever been so disrespectful to anyone, man or woman. But at that moment, I had no inhibitions, and saying what I did filled me with yet more anger and more desire for revenge.

"You cannot behave like this, Ahmad. Go away, there is nothing for you here," my grandmother shouted. This was also the first time I had ever argued with her.

"What do you mean, there's nothing for me here? The apartment is in my name, it's mine, and he has no right to take it away from me. Look at you all," I continued, turning to my aunts and uncles, none of whom had opened their mouths yet. "You should be ashamed, defending this man who's exploiting me, you, everything that passes through his hands, which he gets rid of as soon as he doesn't need it anymore."

I was in such a state that no one responded, no one dared even breathe. I was amazed at myself. I didn't think I was capable of such courage, not in front of my family.

"I'm going up now to my apartment," I said, "the apartment that belongs to me, the one my grandfather built for me. If anyone doesn't agree with me, then they can follow me and stop me, but I warn you, they'll have to step over my dead body. Let me see now if you're really men."

I went out the door, took a deep breath, and headed up the stairs. I heard my father coming behind me. I recognized his heavy footsteps and knew what they meant. I waited for him on the landing, but this time I gave him no chance of hitting me. I kicked him in the belly, sending him crashing against the wall. He came back at me immediately, and I kicked him again and again, sending him back against the concrete wall. An uncle joined in and slapped me across the face. I didn't even know who it was, I was out of my mind with fury and adrenaline, but fortunately he stopped me from continuing.

Suddenly, the full realization of the situation came to me: my father was doubled up in pain, and yet he was still trying to get his hands on me, while my uncle stood between us, looking at me as though he, too, was ready to start beating me. After all, I had just tried to beat up his brother. I turned and started running up the stairs when a door opened, and a hand grabbed me and pulled me into an apartment. It was Aunt Areej, Uncle Mahmoud's wife—at that moment Mahmoud wasn't at home. They had always been supportive of my dance activities. Aunt Areej closed and locked the door behind me and told me I could stay there until things calmed down. It's true that out there, I wouldn't have stood much chance. My father was shouting at the top of his voice in anger and pain, my uncle was trying to break the door down. I waited in there for an hour before I heard them leaving. They were taking my father to the hospital.

When I finally went out, I returned to my grandmother's, but she and my Uncle Omar, my dear uncle confined to his bed, paralyzed, were the only ones left in the apartment.

I went to her, and she started shouting. "You must leave, Ahmad, there is nothing for you here. I don't want to see you ever again!"

"Grandmother, you have stripped us of our rights," I said quietly. "You're on my father's side, and that's why you are throwing us out on the street. If my grandfather were still alive, he would not accept this, and none of this would have happened. But now his soul stands for me and against you all. This will all come back to haunt you. You yourselves will end up homeless, all of you, each of you in a different country, and this house will collapse, it will disintegrate into little pieces, and you'll be on the streets, on your knees, crying out for someone to help you get back on your feet, but no one will help you. I am leaving now, just as you've asked me to, but this tragedy will be yours."

I left the family building after a last look at it. Something was telling me that it was the last time I would see my home standing. I had a strange feeling: I felt as if something were pushing me and my mother away from the family building. I went to my basement school and found my mother waiting for me at the door. She scanned my body to make sure they had not hurt me. I hugged her and started crying. I promised her that I would buy her a house much better than this one and that I would always be the man who would care for her and protect her.

MY MOTHER AND I started living in my basement school, and I continued my studies at the Higher Institute for Dramatic Arts.

I was in the second year there. My mother cooked at her parents' apartment (they lived at the entrance of Yarmouk Camp) and brought the food to the basement. My brother, Amjad, and my sister, Rawan, would join us for meals. Aunt Areej visited us from time to time. Each time, she brought some food.

We lived like this for a month. The end of 2012 was approaching. The vibes of Christmas and New Year's were there. As usual, we celebrated Christmas. In Syria, where people with different religious backgrounds live together, we celebrate feasts of every religion together. So, in the last week of December, we gathered for dinner at my mother's parents' place every evening.

After dinner, Amjad left for the family building. My mother, my sister, and I stayed, enjoying the time together. Then we suddenly heard a huge blast of a bomb, not so far away.

We were all shocked and speechless. The only word my mother said was, "Amjad!"

She ran to her phone and called him. No answer. She then ran toward the door. We feared that it was too dangerous to go out now, so we stopped her. She kept on saying "Amjad, Amjad." Finally, my sister got through to Amjad and shouted, "Amjad is alive!" My mother grabbed the phone from her and spoke to him. She started crying. Then she looked at me with wide, reddened eyes and simply stared at me, scaring me.

"What is it, Ram?"

"It is the building!"

"What do you mean?"

I found out what she meant after sunrise the next morning. My mother and I went to see what had happened. I entered the square of our home. It was in front of our family building where the car bomb had exploded. Everything was completely destroyed: my apartment, my room, my grandfather's apartment, our home—the safety, the warmth, the dreams of my childhood. All the corners of the square, where I used to play with my friends, were full of dust and rubble. The street where I grew up and Uncle Hisham's agency had disappeared.

Many people were running around me. I couldn't recognize their covered faces. They were wearing black and their eyes were full of darkness. They were celebrating something that I did not understand, shooting their guns into the sky.

I looked at the spot where my grandfather used to put his chair. I could see his soul there. I asked him to leave because I didn't want him to see this. My uncles were crying and screaming. I saw Uncle Hisham run toward one of the people shooting into the air, and the man pointed the gun at his face. I ran toward them and stood between them. I could hear my mother shouting "Ahmad, don't!" I knew that Amjad was beside our mother, so I didn't need to fear for her.

As I stood between Uncle Hisham and the man with a gun, the gun was now pointed at my head.

"This is not your country. Get out of here," the man shouted at me.

"This is not your country either. You are the ones who should get out of here," I said. "If you are man enough, shoot me!"

I lifted Uncle Hisham with all my strength and said to him, "Let's go home. Here is our home."

But the gun was still pointed at me. Amjad had covered my mother's eyes. I heard shooting, followed by our mother's scream: "Ahmad!"

"I am alive."

That is the word that came out of me. At the same time, I was asking myself, "Am I alive?"

Cries and screams surrounded me. I couldn't believe what was unfolding in the square. It was so unreal. I kept on wondering if it was a dream. "Can I cry?" I said to myself. "Will tears ever wash the dust away? What is this happening around me? Is it my fault or my destiny?"

So my thoughts went. I felt as if everything in me was destroyed.

SOMEHOW ALL MY family members managed to gather at the house of one of my aunts on the next street. I learned what had happened to Amjad. When the bomb exploded just in front of our family building, he was with our Uncle Omar. They were alone in the building. Everything collapsed around them, though not on them. A huge wardrobe of my grandmother stopped a wall from falling on them. My grandmother had always been saying that she wanted to sell that wardrobe because it was too big and bulky. But she had never done so. Thanks to the unsold wardrobe, Amjad and Uncle Omar survived.

We talked about what we should do now. Each uncle and aunt decided to leave Al-Yarmouk in one way or another. Uncle Hisham asked my father about his family.

My father said to my brother, "Amjad, you stay with your grandmother to support Omar." Then he turned to my sister. "Rawan, you go with your aunt." Finally, he said, "And I will go with my wife and kids to another city."

My mother spoke: "No, Amjad and Rawan should stay with me. I will go to Palmyra."

Uncle Hisham asked me, "And you, Ahmad. What are you going to do?"

"I am OK. I will work it out," I said. "I have to stay in Damascus. I need to get prepared for the dance examination at the institute."

"Thank you for saving my life. You are so brave. I'm sure you will be OK. May God bless you."

I decided to stay in my basement school in Al-Yarmouk. All the other members of the family were leaving for different destinations, some to another city in Syria, others to another country. What was common to us all was that we left everything under the rubble.

Many families had to leave home. This time, they were leaving the Al-Yarmouk camp, not Palestine. Many families had to promise their children and grandchildren that they would come back soon, just as eight-year-old Aisha's family had promised her in 1948. What had happened to little Aisha? Now, at age seventy-two, she had to leave her home again. She could have freed herself from all the promises if she had chosen to do so. She knew the truth, in fact. But this time, too, she chose to keep believing the promise of going back. But to where? Going back to nothing?

Six

A COUPLE OF WEEKS had passed since my home was destroyed by the bomb. After my family members left for different destinations, I continued living in the basement of our dance school in Al-Yarmouk and preparing for the dance exams at the institute.

One Friday morning in the new year, after I'd spent an hour tossing and turning on the mattress, my hand reached for the radio—I needed a bit of music to wake up properly. But I stopped myself just in time, my finger over the play button. The music could attract unwanted attention, and I kept needing to remind myself that the war had come to the neighborhood.

I sighed and ran my fingers through my hair. I did my stretching in silence, as I did every morning, a tried and tested routine of exercises and positions that always managed to sort me out. Slowly I stretched my legs and my back, my neck and arm muscles, and loosened my shoulders. My body started waking up in response to my attention. It was a cure-all.

I was hungry. But food was wishful thinking, and I didn't even open the cupboard. I thought there might be some coffee, but the tin was empty. Angrily, I threw it toward the trash can, but my aim was off. I let it roll on the floor, without worrying about picking it up. Did we have water? Cold water. I took a freezing shower, rubbing myself down as much as possible with the little piece of soap that was left.

I dressed in a pair of jeans and a creased T-shirt, all the clothes I had apart from a sweatshirt that I used as pajamas and my dance tracksuit. I put my hands in my trouser pockets. They were empty.

I had nothing. I was broke.

"When was the last time I even used money?" I asked myself. I couldn't remember. "What am I going to eat? How am I going to manage, with nothing in my pockets?"

I punched the wall and didn't care about the noise. Let the terrorists hear me in this basement school where I had been hiding, like a rat, in the midst of the dark and the dust. I couldn't go on living like this.

I sat on the floor, my back against the wall, my arms wrapped around knees. "Calm down, Ahmad. This isn't the right moment to let yourself be overwhelmed by dejection. You have to dance."

After the bomb destroyed the family home, I felt as if I were a wounded eagle, unable to fly or even breathe. Gradually, however, I felt my life transform, as if losing my home was a turning point for my approach to life. Everything looked different. Even my body movements felt different. Every movement I made was a confirmation that I was still alive. Dancing had become more intense, a mentally deeper experience. My eyes could not cry, but my body did: I sweated out all my tears. As I danced, my spirit would come to me. I felt a fire in me, and I could spread my wings from my back. But this time they were wings of fire. I finally felt that I could breathe and fly again.

A rumble from my stomach told me it was time to get up and get out. I had to look for food. I got to my feet, brushing the dust from my clothes, got my bicycle, and slowly went up the dark, narrow stairs that led to the ground floor. On the street, the sunlight hurt my eyes, so used to the semidarkness of the basement. Gradually the image of the landscape around me took shape—I saw the forms of things. All I could see, under this sharp, blue winter sky, was rubble. Piles of stone, broken cables, metal poles sticking out. Dust and devastation. This was what was left of my material world.

I walked with my head bowed, recalling the sounds of bombs, searching among the rubble for something familiar or something useful, my hands on the handlebar of my bicycle—the road was so ruined and dirty that I couldn't ride on it. I moved slowly, a step at a time, without a precise destination, just making sure I avoided the holes and rocks scattered over the surface.

To think that up until not so long ago, everything around here was living, energized, vibrant. There had been people everywhere, walking along the road or sitting outside the shops, waiting for customers or chatting with the passersby, smoking and drinking, with no cares about the future or about an intolerant God, the one the fanatics use as an excuse for spreading destruction. There were voices and laughter, music and car horns blowing, and then the aroma of tea, spices, and honey. . . .

Another cramp in my stomach reminded me that it was time to stop just thinking about food and find a way of getting some. Hunger was giving me direction. I saw that I wasn't simply wandering the ruined streets of my town—I was heading to my house.

Or to what was left of it. In my daily trips around Damascus, I had always avoided coming back to this area, out of fear of suffering even more. There was nothing left for me in my old neighborhood, apart from nostalgia and regret. But today, there was no choice. So be it—if that was where my heart (or my hunger) was leading me, then I'd better get a move on.

Suddenly, a huge man appeared from behind the sandbags that were used to protect the fighters from bullets during clashes. He waved to me, telling me to get out of the way. So I crossed to the other side of the street. Then he started shooting. Apparently, I had been in his way. He could have shot me instead of risking his life to give me that sign.

"Why? Why am I surviving death every time I face it?" I asked myself. "What is it in my future that needs me to stay alive?"

I got on the bike and pedaled hard, increasing the speed as I approached my destination, dodging cracks and rubble. I slowly recognized what remained of the buildings. Some were completely destroyed, others still stood, but they seemed empty now, and everything was enveloped in an unnatural silence that strangled every bit of hope.

I reached my home. I recognized it only because I knew exactly where it had been, but little remained of its original form. It had been reduced to one wall left standing, supporting a piece of roof and a few stairs here and there. Everything else had collapsed—just large, shapeless blocks of concrete and bent iron rods.

I let the bike fall to the ground and continued on foot. The day of the bomb came back to me in flashes, and I was overwhelmed by anger and sadness, as well as a profound, desperate sense of impotence. I clenched my fists until my knuckles turned white. I had lived in this building since I was born. Together with my relatives, I had built the top floor, one bucket of concrete after another. And then an entire lifetime of work had been destroyed in only a few hours—not just my work, but the work of my family, my uncles and grandparents, and all the other inhabitants of this neighborhood who wanted nothing more than to be left in peace.

Who was responsible? It didn't matter much. The government, the rebels, the extremists, the terrorists. Whoever they were, they were all part of the same structure of violence. Nothing was left of their power games but this pile of dust and rubble. I kicked a lump of concrete. I wanted to shout, attract some attention. I wanted to know if I was the last one left here. Was there anyone I could talk to, share this fate with, search with for something to eat? I sat on a slab of concrete that could have been the floor of my old bedroom. Why had I come back here? What sense did it make? There was no one here to help me. My mother was in Palmyra with my brother and my sister. I had no idea where my father and his woman were, and I didn't want to know. Saeed was in Dubai on tour with the dance company, and . . . his mother. His mother, as far as I knew, was still in Damascus.

I tried calling her, but nothing happened. Not even a dial tone, no reception in the midst of the rubble. I looked at the shell of my old home. Maybe if I climbed to the roof, I could get a signal. I went to the wall of the house, found a little hole for my foot, and pulled myself up. A hold, a foothold, a cable—little by little, I managed to move upward. However hard I tried to find solid pieces to step on, there were no firm places. Although I was scared, I kept going. My hands gripped the concrete; I calibrated my weight, I used my toes. I didn't think of slipping, my body smashing to the ground or being hit by a bullet. I just kept climbing until I reached the top. Sweating, tired, but happy with my achievement.

By looking around from the top, I realized that the devastation was even worse than I had imagined. It was like being in a huge archaeological dig in the midst of the ruins of an ancient civilization worn away by time. It was absurd to think that all this happened so quickly, not because of the natural flow of time but because of the madness of humanity. Wherever I looked, I saw only ruins, silence and death, and a fine dust that burned my eyes and my throat. And yet I was still there, alive.

I had to hurry.

I crouched down to keep myself out of sight. I called again, and this time heard the ring tone. Please, Auntie, I said to myself, please let me hear your voice. Let me hear that you're there, that I'm not destined to be left here alone, to die of hunger.

"Ahmad?" she suddenly answered, her voice sweet music to my ears.

"Auntie, yes, it's me . . . how are you?"

"Finally! Did you want me to die worrying?" she said, almost shouting. "What happened? Why didn't you keep in touch?"

I told her briefly about my situation, and even before I continued, she said, "Get over here right away. You're like a son to me, and we cannot be alone in a time like this. I need you." And she hung up.

I would soon be with her—I'd have shelter and a warm meal, and I'd be able to help her too; we wouldn't be alone anymore in the midst of this solitude and devastation. I couldn't be happier. Or maybe I could—if I had somewhere else to go. If I could manage to leave all this behind me and start again, as far as possible from here. If I could finally find the courage to fly away.

Saeed's parents welcomed me warmly, as if I were their own son. In the beginning, it was just Saeed's mother, her two daughters, and myself who were at home, because Saeed and his father were working elsewhere. I had a room to myself until Saeed came back, along with his aunt and cousins. I began to feel like an intruder, and it didn't seem right to be occupying a room that should really have been given to another family. I had got hold of a tent and decided to move up to the roof, so that I wasn't taking space from anyone but I could still be close to the last friends I had. The truth was, I had no alternative, and I didn't know what I would do without their help. Returning to Al-Yarmouk had become so dangerous that I couldn't go back to my basement school.

It was January and cold, but I did not complain. The only thing that bothered me was having to stay sitting or crouching up on that roof—there were snipers everywhere, and the risk of taking a bullet to the head was real.

"AHMAD? ARE YOU THERE?" someone whispered in the dark outside my tent.

I opened the zipper. It was Saeed, crouching there with two plates in his hands.

"Saeed! Come in, but hurry up. It's cold."

We both laughed, but it was ironic laughter and a little forced, given our situation.

"What have we got this evening?" I asked.

"Rice and potatoes, the house specialty."

"Well . . . at least it's warm."

Since the fighting had started in Damascus, the price of food increased terribly—ten times more than it had been before. Bread, rice, and potatoes were all my new family could afford. If we were lucky, once a month we could treat ourselves to a chicken, to be divided among six of us.

"Have you heard from your mom?" Saeed asked.

"Yes, I finally managed to get hold of her today. She says she'll be back next month, with my brother and my sister. We'll all move to Al-Tadamon, to the house her cousin offered her. It's a small apartment, but if we squeeze up. . . ."

"Better than a tent on the roof. Anyway, I don't understand why she wants to come back to Damascus. Couldn't she stay in Palmyra? At least there she's safe."

"Yes, but she needs to get back to her work in Damascus."

Saeed and I ate the rest of our supper in silence, our eyes fixed on plates that emptied too quickly. When we finished, he was to go back down to his home, to his family. Before he went, I hugged him and thanked him again, as I did every day. His presence now was fundamental for me. I often thought that if it weren't for his constant encouragement, it'd be a terrible struggle to keep going.

"See you tomorrow. Remember, we have to wake up half an hour early to go through the choreography. We won't have time during the day, and the company rehearsals start at four o'clock."

"Of course, Ahmad. Good night."

"Good night to you too, Saeed."

I watched him scuttle toward the stairs and disappear, swallowed up by the darkness. As I did every evening, I piled my things in a corner to free up the mattress and then lay down, pulling the blanket over me. I tried to sleep. The last dance exams at the institute were taking place the next day, and I had to be rested and able to concentrate. But sleep wouldn't come to me.

Although it was cold, I opened the tent flap a little to get a breath of fresh air and escape the impression that above me was just a sheet of plastic. I wanted to see the sky, the scattered stars. I struggled to move a little in the tiny space of the tent . . . and there, before my eyes, was Mount Qasioun. Huge, imposing, illuminated by the moon.

It was a familiar sight, one I'd always known and one that I tried to hold on to so as not to let my past slip away from me. Because I did have a past, even though now that sometimes seemed impossible to me. I lay there, chasing my memories through the rubble of the war, amid the bombing and the fear, until a series of snapshots came to me—as a child, an adolescent, a young man.

DAYS PASSED. My mother returned from Palmyra with Amjad and Rawan. We all moved to the neighborhood of Al-Tadamon, which means "solidarity." It was a very dangerous area, as it was adjacent to Al-Yarmouk, which had been occupied by the terrorists. We rented an apartment from my mother's cousin. It was on the fifth floor. From the window, we could see the rockets being fired into Al-Yarmouk. Each time a bomb blasted, the whole building shook. From that house, we would go to studies or work every day. The war had become the normal condition of our lives. But at least we were together: we lived together, and if we should die, we would die together.

One day, I was standing at a bus stop, waiting for the bus that would take me to the institute. I saw a spark on the ground near me. I knew immediately that the asphalt had been hit by a bullet. I stayed stock-still. Then my phone rang from an anonymous number. I picked up the phone and heard an unknown voice say:

"Don't think we missed you. Next time, we will shoot you in your legs so that you will suffer, wishing for death!"

"Who are you? Hello!" As I spoke, the caller hung up.

That call shocked me. Who was it? Why did they want to do this? On the bus, I received a call from a friend of mine, telling me that I should check my Facebook page, as there was a post calling for my head. I checked my page immediately to find a post with photos of me, with the word "WANTED" printed over them. I deleted the photos and blocked the account responsible for the action.

A week later I received more anonymous calls. One promised to kill my mother; another promised to cut my head off if I kept dancing and teaching dance to kids. I thought that the situation had escalated to such an extent that the police should be alerted, but when I went to them, I was told that they were too busy dealing with bigger matters.

I concluded: "So, it is *my* matter. *I* have to deal with it myself." I went to the old part of Damascus and had the phrase "Dance or Die" tattooed on the precise place on my neck where the blade would fall if I were decapitated. I chose to have the inscription in Hindi to show my respect to Lord Shiva, the dancing god. "A religion based on killing and oppression is not my religion," I reasoned to myself. "My religion is Dance."

So I dealt with my matter. I ensured that, before cutting my head off, the person holding the blade should see my message: "Dance or Die." I had no other choice.

SEVEN

"LISTEN, IT'S A GREAT idea. Just imagine—you'll meet loads of people, you'll have foreign teachers, you'll learn something new, maybe even have a career . . . and in any case, even if you don't win, you've got nothing to lose," Saeed said to me.

"No, but you must be kidding. I can't imagine winning . . . that's not the point," I said.

"So what *is* the point?"

Saeed looked at me and waited for an answer. But I sat staring at the cup in front of me, stirring the dregs of my coffee with a spoon, hoping that I might see there a clearer image of the tangle in my head. I'd have liked to explain to him why I so desperately wanted to take part in a dance reality show. But there was one problem: to participate in the show, I would have to take a year off from the institute.

Saeed and I were in my room in the apartment where I was living with my mother, my brother, and my sister. It was the summer of 2014. We were discussing the announcement of an audition for a television reality show in Lebanon, an Arabic version of *So You Think You Can Dance*.

"Perhaps I just want to get out of here, at least for a while," I said.

"But you have every right to want to leave this place; don't feel guilty about that. I've been away, and your mom has too. I mean, we can't all just hang around here waiting for one another, no?"

From the open window came a breeze that carried with it the usual smell of dust and cement. There was also more light than usual, probably because the previous night they had bombed the building in front of ours, so now its shadow no longer reached the window.

"Yes, but why don't you come too? That would really be great; we'd have a fantastic time together!"

"But what use would I be, Ahmad? They're looking for ballet or contemporary dancers—I'm a break-dancer; what would I do for the audition? A Michael Jackson moonwalk?"

"And why not? You're so good at it."

We both laughed. I watched him get up and take our now-empty cups to the sink. He was right, I knew—of the two of us, I was the right one to respond to the advertisement.

"Well, if you can't manage to decide for yourself, then I'll do it for you. As soon as I get home, I'll send you the link for the application."

He gave me a sweet smile, and I saw once again how fond he was of me. Saeed always knew what was right and wrong for me, and the best thing I could do was to trust him. After all, if it weren't for him, I would have been rotting away, together with all those who, like me, couldn't leave or didn't want to. Just waiting. But for what? For a bomb to fall and destroy this building too?

I had to find the strength to break away from the sick reality that surrounded me. I wanted to leave behind this inexplicable war that stopped us from living daily life, with all its joys and all its problems. I wanted to leave this neighborhood, which the whole world seemed to be watching compassionately, but with no one willing to lift a finger to help us. I wanted to leave this apartment, too small for my mother, my brother, my sister, and me, and so suffocating for people who were too scared to go out into the streets. I wanted to leave this body of mine, which in the mirror was always too thin, which didn't have the right to simply be itself, which had to move and think according to other people's rules. I was tired. I'd been through too much. I wanted to escape and find my own nature, to discover what I really was, without ever having to hide myself away or be ashamed. I even forgot what joy was; I had done all I could to remain. Now it was time to leave.

I looked Saeed in the eye and, without worrying about keeping my voice down, I said: "So be it! I've decided!"

I must have shouted too loudly because I heard noises coming from my mother's room. These days, she was always late coming home, more tired than I'd ever seen her. Saeed and I fell silent, struggling to stifle our laughter, but after a few minutes, our silence was interrupted by a brief cry, a cry of surprise and terror. Terrified, I rushed to the door of her room and threw it open, stirring up a gray cloud that enveloped me and burned my eyes and nose.

"Ram," I said as I coughed, "are you all right?"

As the dust settled, I saw her standing there in front of the mirror, with her hands in her hair. She was completely white, just like every part of her room. The bed, the chest of drawers, the chair with her clothes piled on top of it—everything was covered with a layer of ash and dust. It was a frightening sight—like being in a lifeless place. As long as you stood still, the dust stayed where it was, but the slightest step raised a cloud that floated around the room.

My mother turned toward me, her eyes wide with terror. "What happened? Am I dead?" Her voice was a whisper. I didn't know if she really was confused to the point where she didn't know whether she was dead or alive.

"You're alive, Ram. You're alive and you're fine, Inshallah. The planes came over last night. They destroyed the building opposite. That's what happened." I said, "We are still alive, my beautiful Ram. The destruction is around us, but we should not let it get into us. Look how many times we've survived death. The future is waiting for us, Mom. Aren't you the one who always asks me to stay strong? Be strong, Mom. I love you and I'm here for you."

The fear left her face, but in its place was an empty, resigned expression. Her eyes had never been wearier; they were like those of people who can't go on, who know that all they can do is wait. I watched her reflection in the mirror as she ran her fingers through her hair. I felt Saeed's hand on my shoulder, and I said to myself, more convinced than ever: "I've decided."

The following month, I decided to tell my mother about the reality show. Apart from Saeed, I hadn't spoken to anyone about it. But now it was time to tell her, especially given the phone call I'd just received. I joined her in the kitchen, where she was busy peeling potatoes for supper.

"Ram, can we talk?"

As soon as she heard my voice, she stopped and, without asking any questions, washed her hands and turned to face me. I nodded at the carpet on the floor—it might be a long chat; it was best for us to sit comfortably.

"Listen, Ram, I've done something. Don't worry—it's nothing bad."

My mother knew immediately that it was something important. She leaned the top half of her body toward me, as if to hear better what I had to tell her.

"Right. On the spur of the moment—well, also because I thought a lot about it—I applied for something that'll mean I have to be away from you for a while. Not too much, though. At the most a couple of months and then I'll be back and . . . "

I struggled to get the words out of my mouth, heavy as they were. I didn't want my mother to worry about me, at least not as much as I worried about her.

"Ahmad, are you sure you're all right? What's all this mystery about? Something, far from here . . . what is it you have to go and do?"

In the end, all my reticence proved counterproductive—my mother was looking at me with an expression not just of worry, but of terror. I had to hurry and tell her everything, or else she'd have a heart attack. Or perhaps maybe I'd have one, given how violently my heart was beating. My mouth had become too dry to speak, so I got up, filled two glasses of water, gave one to my mother, and gulped mine down instantly. I breathed deeply and said, "I sent an application to take part in a television show about dancing." I directed my gaze at the bottom of the empty glass.

She said nothing and didn't move an inch. I lifted my head slowly—she was staring at me. Or rather, she was observing me, searching for something that she didn't seem able to find, or something she had found, something she'd always known. She half-closed her eyes and smiled, a smile I knew well, which dated back to years ago. She leaned back, with one hand on the floor and the other spread over her knee.

"Was that really so difficult to tell me? You gave me a fright. It's an excellent idea, Ahmad. It seems perfect for you. And where is this show?"

"In Beirut."

"That's not even so far away. But what about your graduation?"

"I can take a year off from my education. I took one off for work already, but I can still take another. The institute allows up to a two-year extension. So, that's it."

"OK. But then, promise me that you will graduate. And when will you hear from the television show?"

"They've already replied. They've just called me. I've been accepted."

She leaned toward me with her arms open. I let her hug me, and I rested my head on her chest.

"But this is wonderful. And why aren't you jumping for joy?"

"Well, it's a bit early to be celebrating. For the moment, all that happens is an audition, and if that goes well, they'll decide whether to let me take part in the program or not."

"But it's great news anyway. Just think of how many people will have tried, and out of them all, they've chosen you. That's already a victory, no?"

"Yes, but . . . "

"What's the problem, Ahmad?"

My mother untangled herself from our hug. With one hand, she gently held my chin and turned it toward her, forcing me to look her in the eye. We sat there motionless, just a few inches from each other, for I don't know how long.

"It's not because it's in Lebanon, is it? Do you feel guilty because you have to leave?"

I lowered my head slightly, giving her the answer she was looking for.

"Listen. If I could, I'd leave this place too. Right now, immediately. I haven't left only because I don't want to leave you to face this hard life by yourself. I want you and your brother and sister to graduate from your universities and get your diplomas. Then I will be happy."

I knew my mother was on my side, and I had to do something good, make my way in life, to thank her for everything she'd always done for me.

"I know, Ram, it's stupid, but I still can't manage to really celebrate, and for as long as I'm here, things won't change. Do you know that just before—" I began to laugh. "Just before, when the call came from that program, they were recording it, they record them all so as to let people hear the joyous reactions of successful applicants. So they explained everything and told me I'd been selected, and I just went: 'OK.' OK, and that was it."

Now my mother laughed too, thinking of how my lack of enthusiasm must have disappointed the program's producers. Then, when we'd calmed down, I added a last little detail: "But there's a problem. How can I go to Lebanon without a passport?"

I had a valid travel document issued for stateless travelers like myself. But applying for a visa to another country based on this document was no longer a simple matter. For dance tours, the dance company had been able to get me a visa through its special connections to influential people in each country. I myself did not have such special connections in Lebanon. Besides, after the civil war broke out in Syria, all Arabic countries became more restrictive in giving visas to stateless refugees here. Even inside Syria, the movements of stateless refugees had become restricted. So it was impossible for me to obtain a visa to Lebanon.

"Listen: Ask them directly, no? Maybe, since they work in television, they'll know how to sort these things out."

"You're right, Ram. That's what I'll do."
"Do you still have doubts about me being always right?"
So I wrote an email to the show:

From: ahmadj@****.com
To: humanresources@****.lb
Subject: 040490 entrance visa

Good morning,

My name is Ahmad Joudeh and my reference number is 040490, which your staff gave me yesterday during our phone call.

I'm writing now about a bureaucratic complication that I have to sort out: I was born in Syria, in Damascus, but my family on my father's side are of Palestinian origin. This means that for Syria I am Palestinian and I didn't receive Syrian nationality at birth, but I haven't been able to obtain Palestinian nationality because I was born in Syria. I am therefore stateless and have no passport. Under the current conflict, it means I won't be able to cross the border and take part in the auditions that you have kindly invited me to.

I'd like to ask you if you know anything of the necessary procedure for obtaining a visa suitable for my case, or if you have any information that might help me in this way. Taking part in your program is something I really want to do and I really don't want to give up on it for any reason.

Thank you for your attention.

Yours,

Ahmad Joudeh

And I quickly heard back:

From: humanresources@****.lb
To: ahmadj@****.com
Subject: Re: 040490 entrance visa

Good morning Ahmad,

Unfortunately, this sort of situation is very common . . . unlike your application, which stood out among all those sent to us: we were very impressed by it and for this reason we all hope to have you with us on the program.

The procedure for obtaining a visa without a passport, as you can imagine, complicates things greatly, but it doesn't mean it's impossible.

Rest assured we'll do everything possible to get you over here, contacting the embassies directly. Don't worry, we'll take care of everything and we'll find a solution. We'll let you know as soon as we have some news.

In the meantime, don't hesitate to get in touch if you have any further questions or news for us.

Yours sincerely,

Human Resources
So You Think You Can Dance Arabia

But this positive news was followed a month later with a disappointing email:

From: humanresources@****.lb
To: ahmadj@****.com
Subject: Re: 040490 entrance visa

Dear Ahmad,

We're sorry to have to inform you that unfortunately our attempts to get you a visa for Lebanon have failed. We contacted both the Syrian consulate and the Ministry of Labor, but to no avail. It's a real pity—we so much wanted to give you an opportunity to take part in the auditions, not only because of your obvious talent, but because your story, through our program, would have had a big impact on our viewers.

The only possible solution now is for you yourself to manage to get a visa, but we're aware of how complex and difficult this is. Please let us know if there are any further developments in this direction.

We obviously remain open to the possibility of offering you all the help we can and we'll keep your contact details so that we can inform you of any potential future collaboration.

Yours sincerely,

Human Resources
So You Think You Can Dance Arabia

No visa. I wouldn't be leaving the country this time, wouldn't be leaving this hell. I felt stupid for having hoped it might happen, for having believed that things might really change for me. "What should I tell Saeed now? And my mother? They are already imagining me on television. They think I might really make a mark, do something really great. But instead I am destined to stay here and rot, to drown slowly in this ocean of desperation. No! I will focus on my graduation. And after that, who knows what life has in store for me."

I was so busy sorting out my thoughts that it took me a while to realize my cell phone was ringing. On the display was a number I didn't recognize.

"Good morning, is that Mr. Ahmad Joudeh?"

"Yes, it's me. Who is this?"

"My name is Abbas. I'm working on a new show." He mentioned the name of a well-known singer. "I was given your number by the Higher Institute for Dramatic Arts in Damascus. I'm looking for dancers for some pieces we'd like to include in the concert. Are you interested?"

Was this some sort of joke?

"Yes, of course, I'd be very interested. When?"

"Auditions will be in a month's time, here in Beirut, and then the rehearsals will start right away. Our choreographer has everything ready."

"Beirut?"

Someone was making fun of me. Someone who knew my story and decided to have a good laugh at my expense. It was the only explanation for this absurd coincidence. My hopes were dashed—another opportunity down the drain.

"That's right, yes," this Abbas person continued. "The rehearsals are here in Beirut, and then the tour is around Lebanon."

"I have to stop you there. I would jump at the chance if I could, but because I'm stateless, I have no passport. I have only a travel document for refugees. So I can't leave Syria."

How many times did I have to utter that sentence? Hundreds, probably. I'd stopped counting.

"Ah, but that won't be a problem. I told you who we're working for, no? He always manages to solve this sort of problem very quickly. You have no passport because you're a refugee, right? Palestinian?"

Was this possible? Did he really just say that, or was I hearing voices?

"Yes. I mean, I was born here in Syria, but my late grandfather came from Palestine. It's him who was the Palestinian refugee."

"Perfect. Let me have your email address so that I can send you the contract. You sign it and send it back by email, all right? Our client is a great supporter of your cause. Believe me, he's already helped several people in your situation."

My hand holding the phone began to tremble. I had to put the phone on the table and switch on the speaker. We agreed on a few last arrangements, and after a series of phrases like "thank you" and "see you soon" and "I'm counting on it," I hung up and let myself fall against the back of the chair. I threw my head back, my eyes to the ceiling, my mouth open in a smile. I'd managed it, this time. I'd managed it.

I had to tell someone. I had to tell everyone. I opened my laptop and went on Facebook. I updated my timeline: "Dear friends, I am happy to announce that I will soon be going to dance in Lebanon. Inshallah."

I switched everything off and grabbed my bike and headed for Saeed's house—he had to be the first to know about this incredible event. It was almost as though it couldn't be true until I shared it with him. I pedaled quickly through the dusty streets, leaving a little wake of sand behind me. The sky, the sun, the buildings that were still standing and those that were already in ruins, the tired but unvanquished eyes of the few people I passed—everything today seemed to be in harmony. Everything danced around me; everything was in equilibrium and in movement; I saw that everything changes, dies, and is reborn, that everything lives as it has never lived before. Just like me.

"CONE OR A CUP?"

"Cone," I said to Saeed as I looked for my wallet.

It was a month later. We had come out into town to celebrate the great news, greater news than we had ever expected—proof of the fact that the force of life manages to achieve its ends along paths completely unforeseeable. I finally got granted a visa to Lebanon, thanks to the Lebanese singer who was interested in having me in his show. That had opened the door for me to go to Beirut to participate in the audition for *So You Think You Can Dance Arabia*. We were in the Al-Hamidiyah souk, walking down its long corridors full of colorful stalls, breathing in the various aromas, and heading toward the Umayyad Mosque. The many hundreds of people who'd come outdoors on this splendid September day were all around us, all with their own things to do and their own problems to solve, while we sauntered, enjoying every instant of our moment of celebration.

Saeed and I were talking about the director of the show for the Lebanese singer. After taking the trouble to help me get a visa to Lebanon, he had decided I should not be part of their show.

"But why was the director so upset? I really don't understand it," Saeed said, licking a drop of ice cream running down his wrist.

"Because he's a miserable man—he was after some free publicity, and I didn't give it to him, that's why."

"But you weren't obliged to do it, were you? I mean, it's your Facebook page, and you can write what you want on it."

"Mmm . . . but maybe I made a mistake too. They'd asked me to keep a low profile, and instead. . . . Just as well this all happened *after* I got the visa. But the good thing is that the visa is mine now, and they cannot void it. It's a visa for three months, so I can use it for the competition."

"Just as well, really. But I still think that firing you because of an internet post is a bit over the top."

"Well, I let myself get carried away by my enthusiasm, and the post was a bit stupid. I could have waited . . . and perhaps even explained why I was going to Lebanon to dance. But in the end, it was the singer's production people who got me the visa."

Saeed laughed.

"Well, in the end maybe it's better, no?"

He gave me a big smile, full of sincere happiness. Yet again I realized how important he was for me. If it hadn't been for him, I wouldn't be here now eating ice cream and talking about what was best—I'd be home alone, going stir-crazy and fretting about the worst-case scenario.

"For sure, it's better this way. Dancing on tour with a singer in Lebanon is great, but there's no comparison with taking part in a television program, is there?"

"And then even people abroad see these programs; it'll really boost your visibility. You know there's an American on the jury?"

"I know, I know. I know everything, but I don't want to think about it because then I get too excited!"

We came to the end of the souk and left the darkness of the gallery, to be overwhelmed by light reflected off the stone of the Roman temple of Jove and off the immense Umayyad Mosque—a light so intense and dazzling that I could barely keep my eyes open. We laughed as we pretended to bump into the passersby, just as we used to when we were kids.

Saeed exclaimed, "I propose a toast to the poor director and his poor show, a poor director who fires anyone he doesn't like, and thus our hero finds himself with a work visa and an invitation to take part in—drumroll—*So You Think You Can Dance!*"

"Shhh, idiot! Don't say these things out loud, with all these people around."

"Aw come on, Ahmad, chill. No one here is going to fire you," he said and then burst out laughing. He held out his cone to me, and I touched it gently with mine, and so we toasted the great news.

Saeed did all he could to show his enthusiasm, but there was a touch of melancholy in the air. The happiness was all mine, and it wasn't fair. I would be leaving him behind in the midst of the ruins; I would put thousands of miles between us. I couldn't not feel guilty about this. I took his hand and dragged him away from the square, running among the people. We came to a little side street, an alley between two rows of buildings. I leaned back on the wall and pulled him toward me.

"Saeed, you've always done a lot for me. I want to promise you something—one day, I'll repay you for all this. I'll find a way to pull us out of here, together, and we'll go somewhere else, somewhere where we can be free and happy. I have nothing now, but one day I'll manage it, believe me."

We were so close, I could see his eyes shining. We looked at each other in silence for a few seconds, seconds that lasted an eternity. Then Saeed said, "Listen, I'm not friends with you just to have something in return. And in any case, I'll only accept your promise if you promise me something else."

"Just tell me; tell me what you want."

"You must promise me that you'll get through this audition, that you'll take part in the program, and that you'll win it."

"I promise, Saeed. I'll do it. I'll do it for us."

With my eyes filling up with tears, I threw my arms around his neck. I hugged him and he hugged me in return, while the late summer breeze ruffled our hair.

Then we separated and, smiling, left the alley. We immersed ourselves in the crowds of the souk and walked until we came out on the Al-Thawra road, where we picked up our bicycles and headed home, pedaling slowly so as to be together right up to the very last moment.

FROM FAR AWAY, Beirut was a collection of sparkling lights that stood out against the dark of the night. Completely at a loss, I let myself be carried along by the flow of the other travelers; I went where they went, I pulled out my documents when they pulled theirs out. Then, once I got off the rickety bus that had taken us across the border, the other participants from Damascus and I looked for a taxi to take us to the hotel where we'd be staying for the near future.

Only now, in the taxi, did I begin to realize where I was.

We rushed through the city streets, my eyes glued to the window. The buildings were extravagantly shaped, and so tall and out of proportion that they looked as though they were about to collapse, but at the same time they gave me a sense of stability I'd never felt before. They were so sinuous that I wouldn't have been surprised if, all of a sudden, they actually moved. Covered in glass, mirrors, and steel, they were completely different from the concrete blocks of Al-Yarmouk.

The quietness in Beirut was scary for me. There were no sounds of bombs or rifle shots, which was weird. But I was fascinated by the beauty of the city: the colors! Of every type, every shade, matte and gloss, all melding with one another in the speed of our journey, merging with the lights that I had trouble distinguishing individually—the yellow of streetlights; the white of car and motorbike lights; the green, yellow, and red of traffic lights; the blue of entry phones; the red of stop signs—colors everywhere, wherever my eyes came to rest, erupting out of the windows, reflected on the sidewalks, blaring from the advertising billboards, creating a multicolored vortex of ceaseless amazement.

"This is it," the taxi driver said suddenly, and his voice almost made me jump.

Before I was even out of the taxi, he'd unloaded our suitcases. "There, look, over there. That's your hotel," he said.

He pointed to the other side of the road. We paid him, and as I'd been told to do, I asked the others to give him a tip. Lebanese pounds were less colorful than Syrian pounds. They looked greenish, like the American dollars I'd seen in movies.

As the taxi disappeared into the busy traffic, I felt truly on the ground in Beirut—all my weight pressed down, as though on arrival my first desire was to leave my footprint. I took a deep breath and smelled the strong, salt smell of the sea. For a moment, I thought about calling for another taxi to take me there, to touch it, even to dive into the water. But it was night, I had my suitcase with me, and I didn't have enough money, and the next day was going to be a tough day. "Best take a rain check for now; after the audition, I can walk to the beach," I thought.

But I really didn't feel like rushing to lock myself away in the hotel. I sat on the edge of a big potted plant and looked around, giving myself the gift of a few more minutes in the open air. It was late, but there were still plenty of people around, walking or passing in cars—men and women of all ages wearing shirts, T-shirts, jeans, sandals, sneakers. No sign of any hijabs, kaffiyehs, *bishts*; no traditional garb with any sort of link to religion. On the advertising poster in the window of a pharmacy next to me, there was even a photograph of a naked woman (or at least she seemed naked), busily massaging her face with a moisturizing cream.

A little farther on, there was a sushi restaurant. And then bars, banks, clothing stores.

It was not the first time I had been to Beirut. I had been there with the company to perform at the Ba'albak Festival before the civil war broke out in Syria. Beirut hadn't changed. But this time, I felt it was another world, as this was the first time I had traveled after the war. I had come here for the opportunity of change: a change of air, a change of custom, a change of everything. Even sitting beside this plant and looking around made me feel freer. This city had much to offer me—I could feel it. It was up to me to make the most of it.

I got to my feet again, and a little shiver of happiness ran down my spine. I'd gladly have spent the whole night out there, but it was time for bed. The next few days were critical for my future, and the best thing to do was to be ready for them, rested and in a peaceful frame of mind.

Goodnight, Beirut. Thanks for letting me come this far.

THE FLOOR CREAKED under my feet as they pushed down, as if I were about to set off on a sprint. My toes pushed and the joints contracted, my ankles cracked, and my knees bent under my weight as I took up my position. Before me were a few stairs, cast in darkness. I'd have to be careful about when I entered the stage and, farther on, the blinding glare of the spotlights. The judges sat to the left; behind them was the audience and to the right was a wall with the program's name and logo.

I'd spent hours in a sort of waiting room, together with others like me who were on a quest for their big break. We were all very different from one another, coming from different countries in the Arab world and with different dance styles, and yet the same light burned in our eyes: the desire to take this chance, to see how it would work out, to pursue our passion. Technicians and production assistants stood beside us in this long, narrow room with high walls. They each had a little radio that kept them in contact with the directors, and they arranged the order in which the contestants were to audition.

The closer my moment for going on stage, the more intensely my memories of the past came to life and flowed through me. I thought of all the times when I had been unsure of myself, when I thought I'd never make it. The people who'd hindered me came to mind—everything returned, from the slaughter of the sheep at the wedding to saying good-bye to my mother before setting off for Beirut. It was as if I could see a single thread running through all the twists and turns that had brought me here.

I shook my head, as though to free it of these thoughts. I needed to concentrate. I'd already warmed up, so I kept rotating my ankles and wrists in movement, stretching my back and touching my toes. My legs trembled. "Just keep still, you two," I said to them. "I need all your collaboration now. No funny business, please. This isn't the right moment to start goofing around. My life is on the line right now, right here. My future. We don't want to ruin it all simply because we can't handle our nerves, do we?"

I'd just sat down again when a crackling sound came from a radio of one of the technicians. He came over to me, put a hand on my shoulder, and said, "You're up," pushing me slightly to get me on my feet. I jumped like a jack-in-the-box.

"Come on, it's your turn. Go out to the center of the stage and take up your position on those white marks."

"Here we go." I left my thoughts in the waiting room and walked, straight and determined, toward my objective. I felt light, as though my feet weren't touching the floor at all, but floating in the air. I was impalpable, disembodied, pure spirit. That's good, I thought, moving toward the microphone. I'd be able to jump higher.

I had wanted to dance barefoot, but at the last moment, I decided I'd keep my shoes on—I didn't know the stage, and the floor might be slippery. Best to avoid any surprises. I walked to the center with the best posture I could muster. The first impression was fundamental. I stopped before the microphone on its stand; the spotlights were on me. I could hear the audience chattering, but I couldn't see them, at least not as well as I could see the judges. They asked me my name and where I was from; I answered politely but without giving much detail on my origins. I knew how people would react when they heard Al-Yarmouk mentioned, and I didn't want to play that game—I was here as a dancer, not as a refugee. But as soon as they simply heard the name of my neighborhood, they were startled and started looking at me in a different way. After all, it couldn't have gone any other way.

"Why do you dance?" one of the judges asked, as soon as she realized that my life had been buried under rubble.

I responded with the simple truth: "I dance to escape from the horrors of life and to find its sweetness once more."

The war had taken everything from me, everything except my own self. And dance was so deeply rooted in me, nobody could take it away. I danced to express what I couldn't explain in words; I danced to sweat away my tears; and with every movement I screamed out my pain, not waiting for an echo. I danced to feel alive and to exist.

A tracking spotlight switched on. It picked me out, and that was my cue. As the music, Sting's "Desert Rose," started, so did my body, following a choreography that I'd worked on tirelessly and which I had learned by heart. My right leg rose up the line of my left leg, with no need for me to tell it to do so. It crossed behind my left leg and spun me; it kicked forward and my pelvis followed. My arms reacted to this impulse, and my hands accompanied them, sliding through the air, making every movement wider and lighter. My body was in unison—a sum of parts that moved in complete harmony. Here and now, I existed. From the tips of my toes to the tips of my fingers, what the judges saw was what I really was. And my history danced with me—a grand jeté for every time I'd been told not to dance; an arabesque, tight and firm, for all those who humiliated me; a pirouette for every time I'd risked death because of a stupid war. Take a look at me now, all of you, I was saying. Do I look as though I've been weakened by your threats? Do you think my head is bowed with the weight of your weapons? Perhaps from tomorrow on, my life will be even more complicated, and your hatred for me will be even more violent. But if only for today, I am the Fire.

I stopped in my closing position. There was nothing but silence in my head, a profound sense of peace, but from the theater came a deafening noise. Applause. I felt as if I'd come back from a different dimension. I looked at the audience, I looked at the judges, and all of them looked at me.

"You are unique, there on the stage. I see you have self-confidence; you believe in what you're doing and that makes you happy. It's as though you're flying rather than dancing. I'm so pleased to come across a talent like yours," was the first judge's comment.

"When you move your hands, you look like a bird searching for peace. Your body is made for dancing," the second judge said.

And last of all, Pierre Dulaine, a famous dance coach, a former dancer himself, Palestinian in origin but a naturalized American, said "Bravo! Bravo! Bravo! For a tall gentleman, you use all of your body. All of it! You fly through the air. And you are flying, looking for freedom. I have tears in my eyes because he is Palestinian," he said to the other judges. "He has had problems before, and now he also has problems in Syria. I am so sorry," he concluded, sending me a kiss.

They accepted me for the show. The decision was unanimous. It went exactly as I thought it would go, because I had known that once I'd come this far, it couldn't have gone any other way. This wasn't presumption, but rather a sense of destiny—I knew there was no alternative for me. I felt serene, as though every piece was finally in the right place, as though all the mechanisms of my life had started working properly. And this, incredible as it seemed, was just the beginning.

"HAVE YOU SEEN HIM? He never gets changed. Always wearing the same clothes."

"Maybe he's poor?"

"But haven't you heard? Didn't you know he's from Damascus?"

"It's worse than that . . . he's from Al-Yarmouk. You know, where the Palestinians are."

refugee / re-fyu̇-ˈjē / noun—A person who has been forced to leave their country in order to escape war, persecution, or natural disaster. "Tens of thousands of refugees fled their homes."

So the dictionary defines a refugee. But I hadn't fled. I was born a refugee.

The live shows would start in a few weeks. The contestants were receiving lessons from the choreographers so that the latter would get to know them. It is difficult to keep a secret in a dance rehearsal room—the whispered words and stifled laughter, together with the knowing looks, traveled rapidly, reflected through the mirrors until they reached their target. I knew my colleagues didn't like me. I knew they were making fun of me, especially the hip-hop dancers in their solid little gang, drawing strength from all their designer clothes and, more than anything else, from their Lebanese passports. They were performing at home and felt as though they had the right to inflict any sort of injustice, as long as they came out on top.

Today Ivana, one of the choreographers, had us practicing the cha-cha. It was the first time I'd tried this dance, and I already felt stupid because I couldn't really figure out how to move. All I wanted was to avoid those four bullies making fun of me—that really could send me over the top. I hid myself at the back of the room, away from their looks, and concentrated on the dance, studying the steps and learning the choreography by heart, trying to see myself while I danced and thinking about how I could loosen up my movements a bit.

"Hey, you! Lead me and show them how it's done."

There was no doubt about it—Ivana was speaking to me. She wanted me to be her partner and to lead her, in front of the rest of the class. It was the last thing I wanted, but I had no choice. She took my hand, and I started moving with her, trying to appear confident and at ease.

"See? He's leading me perfectly. That's what you all have to do."

It worked! I really didn't know how, but I must have danced well enough to receive those compliments from Ivana—she was a kind and enthusiastic choreographer, but she never said more than she needed to. The other dancers looked at me with a slightly puzzled air, even though I was more surprised than they were. "Perhaps from now on they'll appreciate me a bit more. Or perhaps not. Perhaps they'll hate me now not just because I'm a Palestinian refugee, but because I'm trying to show that I'm worth something," I said to myself. But in the end, what did it matter? I was there to do a job, no more than that. I met all their gazes with a sincere, guileless smile—I had nothing against anyone, least of all my partners in this adventure. I learned some time ago that hatred is best fought with love.

I would not wait for those who hurt me to apologize, or even to recognize that they hurt me, because they would never understand, they would never know. So I just let them be and left.

After the lesson was over, we had a two-hour break before the afternoon courses. I didn't have any friends there yet—staying at the studio meant being alone again, sitting in a corner. Perhaps things would change gradually. Perhaps, as time went by, I'd develop a real relationship, a bit of solidarity and respect with some of the others. But as things stood, that wasn't happening, so I preferred taking a walk alone to get some fresh air.

I gathered my things and went out, heading along the roads of the old town, with its gray and beige buildings that made me think of home. I missed it and I didn't miss it, Al-Yarmouk, even though it seemed as if it would always be with me. I'd never be free of its presence; it was like some sort of brand, as if the place where I was born said everything about me and my life.

I wandered, lost in my thoughts, until I realized that I'd come to the sea—a great stretch of water that seemed to embrace the city with a sort of maternal sweetness, as though seeking to console all its inhabitants, one by one. It was exactly what I needed at that moment.

I went down to the beach and took off my shoes, letting the soft sand caress my feet. I slowly moved to the water's edge and lifted my eyes—there was a concert of big white and dark clouds up there, all moving with the wind, chasing and covering one another. It was as though the whole horizon were gathering, about to cry.

A thunderclap roared, dark and deep, like the echo of a bomb arriving from far away. I was lost in my thoughts. *If I close my eyes, I can clearly see the smoke, the ash, the ripped flesh, the bodies piled up at the sides of the roads. If I squeeze them shut even more, I can see my room, or rather all the rooms I've ever lived in, because I'm a refugee even within my own family—a freak of nature, someone who quite simply doesn't have and will never have his own place in the world. So many wars have I lived through—my own and those of others. How many injustices have I had to bear in silence, without ever rebelling? Because this is the refugee's condition—born on the wrong side, they must keep their mouths shut and do no more than thank those who allow them to remain alive, even though those same people condemn them to an infernal existence. A refugee can't ask for justice, because a refugee is someone who is already serving a sentence. As if the war were our fault.*

Aren't we all refugees in this life? Aren't we all guests? No one lives forever; each of us seeks refuge and safety in someone else's home or heart; every one of us has his own war.

My war started when I decided to be a dancer.

Heedless of the approaching storm, I continued walking, one step after another, until the water at my ankles was at my calves, my knees, my waist. The waves gently rinsed the tiredness out of me, the physical tiredness from the dance lessons and the tiredness I felt every day in my attempts to show others that, despite my origins, I was like them—a young guy who dreams and fights to live in a free and happy world, above all a world free of prejudice. A person, a human being.

The sea welcomed me into its embrace. I dived into the water and lay there floating on the surface, cradled by its sweet movements. "I am alive and I am here"—nothing more mattered to me. I closed my eyes and waited for the rain to come soon, plenty of it, to wash my soul.

The rain started to fall. At first just the occasional small drop, then bigger drops closer together, and then it was as if the sky had split in two to allow a waterfall to descend, a waterfall it had been holding up there for who knows how long. I lifted my head skyward and opened my arms in gratitude, accepting it all—the water from the sea beneath me and the water from the sky above.

It ran over my face, over my back and my chest, it caressed my legs, it danced around my arms. It disinfected my wounds. It helped me forgive myself for all the hurt I had caused myself, for everything I'd allowed others to do to me, without ever raising my voice. And I resolved to do this every day, to stop myself from dwelling on the pain and to concentrate only on the good that, all things considered, this damaged life had managed to give me.

If anyone had seen me now, dancing and jumping under the rain in the midst of the sea, still dressed, they'd have thought I was mad. But I never felt so alive and happy. I needed the water.

"SO, HOW'S IT GOING? We always watch you on television. We're cheering you on," Saeed said to me on the phone.

"Everything's fine. The city is great, and the choreographers are really good. I'm learning lots of things."

"But?"

"No, nothing. It's just a bit difficult at times."

"What? Is the level too high?"

"No, no, that's not it. The other day, they even offered me a five-year contract."

"But that's wonderful—well done! Five years . . . that's a long time."

"Yes, I turned it down."

"What? Are you crazy?"

"No, it's just that as you say, it's a long time. I want to go back to Damascus and finish my studies, I don't want to do television shows. These people aren't interested in me; they're interested in my story."

"Is that why you say it's difficult at times?"

"Well, a bit, yes. It's as though the producers are only interested because I increase the audience share. And with the others on the show, things are really hard. I don't know if it's envy, racism, or what, but there's a big gap between us. The only people who are kind to me are the choreographers. And the judges."

"And don't forget the audience. The people in the studio and all of us at home. Perhaps you're too close to it all to realize, but the fact that you're on that program is becoming a big thing around here. People are paying attention to you; they believe in you. You're helping a lot of people."

"What?"

"Think about it, Ahmad—you're not the only Palestinian in the world, and you're not the only refugee. I mean, not just in Syria, but in all the Arab countries. There are thousands of people who see you as an icon. You've become a symbol of redemption for people. They want to see you win. And they want to win with you, for once in their lives."

"But . . . you really think so? Really?"

"Well, maybe I was wrong to tell you. You sound nervous now."

"A little bit, yes. But it's also satisfying. Knowing that I'm doing something good not just for myself, but for others too."

"Exactly, that's the way to look at it—this place is full of people rooting for you and transmitting energy. Is that better?"

"Yes, I'd say that's much better!"

"What are you up to today?"

"Classes. Hip-hop."

"Ha! You too now?"

"Let's say I try to get by. I don't think I have the right style."

"Of course you do, don't worry about it. It's not true that hip-hop is all posing; you need to know how to move, and you have no problem with that."

"In any case, I could do with some lessons."

"Of course, I'll take care of that when you come back. Go to your classes and keep yourself focused on them."

"I will, I promise. Bye, Saeed, thanks for calling."

"Don't mention it . . . the least I could do."

"Saeed . . . I miss you."

"I miss you too."

THE QUARTERFINALS OF *So You Think You Can Dance* were in December 2014. Several diplomats from the Palestinian embassy came, as well as my mother and Saeed (as Syrian nationals, they could travel to Lebanon without a visa—I was not, as only a father can pass on nationality in Syria, as in other countries in the Arab world). Everyone was expecting me to win, and the tension was high, to the point that when I heard "No," based on the vote of the judges, there was almost a revolt in the studio—people in tears, fans trying to join me on stage, shouts and insults for the judges and their decision. Nobody was happy that I didn't get through to the finals. By that point, I had a solid group of supporters, both at home and in the studio. Important people had come to Beirut just to see me dance live, and objectively I knew that I didn't deserve to be eliminated. And just as I knew, everyone knew—all the other contestants, the audience, even the judges themselves, deep down, knew.

And yet, faced with that verdict, I wasn't upset. The presenter of the show gave me the microphone to say my last words.

"Who could overcome all the difficulties I have faced and reach this stage? Today will not be my end; today is the beginning!" I said, smiling, and I left the stage. But in the wings, all hell was waiting for me—the security staff had to intervene to escort me from the stage area, separating me from the excited audience and the journalists, who were already trawling for news.

"Do you think what has happened is fair? . . . The Palestinian ambassador is present; do you have anything to say about that? . . . Do you know if there are political reasons behind your elimination?"

I didn't know. I didn't even want to respond, I just wanted to see my mother, and that was the only thing I shouted to the security staff. "The woman with blond hair sitting in the front row—please bring her to me."

They made us wait for ages in the dressing room—my mother, Saeed, and me. We sat there in silence, with nothing to say, each lost in our own thoughts—my mother was sad, Saeed was angry, and I was confused but strangely satisfied, as I'd managed to realize my dream and to take my dancing out of the confines of Al-Yarmouk. It was only hours later, when the broadcast was over, when the dancers who were still in the contest had returned to the hotel on buses provided by the production team and the audience had left the studio, that they finally let us out.

We went back to the hotel, avoiding a sea of journalists thirsty for gossip and news. We were having dinner and making jokes while the phone in the room rang continually. Had it been up to me, I wouldn't have answered, but my mother took care of all that—more out of good manners than anything else. She told them all that I had no statement to make, said good-bye, and hung up. Then came one call where she gestured to me to come closer. She covered the mouthpiece with her hand and whispered:

"It's the hotel reception; they say Pierre Dulaine is downstairs and he'd like to see you. Do you want to?"

Dulaine, one of the judges, had always been very sweet and kind to me, and he'd made it clear from the very beginning that he believed in my talent. I said yes immediately.

I went down to the foyer, and as soon as I saw him he said, with a serious expression on his face, "Ahmad, don't be sad because of what's happened. You're a great dancer; you don't need them to prove it. I just wanted to say I'm sorry."

"But you don't need to be sorry; it doesn't matter. It was great experience. I did all I could."

"Exactly, you did all you could, and you did it well. You didn't deserve to go out."

"So why am I out?"

He did not reply immediately. An embarrassed silence set in between us. I kept my eyes on the floor.

Finally, he said, "I'm sorry, how things went. I came to tell you that I don't want you to think it was your fault."

And then he left, in silence.

The television show asked me to stay on one more week in Beirut, to appear onstage during the last episode. When the program finished, the producer said good-bye to all the contestants one by one, but she never came to me. They dismissed me with a seven-hundred-dollar voucher to buy some dance clothes. Pierre gave me his laptop computer as a present. They also offered me a job as a dancer on another show, but I still hadn't completed my studies and, with the impression that the world of television had made on me, I wasn't keen on the idea.

In the days following the elimination, I had all the time in the world to think about what happened. I abandoned all such thoughts in Beirut before getting in a taxi that was to take me home.

When I arrived in Damascus, I immediately felt relieved, ready to begin new adventures. One thing I learned from this experience was that I didn't have to win everything in life. For me, it was enough to see my mother and Saeed laughing happily and giving me all this care and love, with all the people who believed in me. Being loved is the source of my strength. There was, however, just one doubt that continued to buzz insistently in my head. If, after everything that had happened, my destiny wasn't what I imagined—winning *So You Think You Can Dance*—then what did life have in store for me?

EIGHT

BACK HOME, I FELT as if the place had changed. The war wasn't over; in fact, it was worse. But after four years I had grown used to it. Any anomaly, if you experience it for long enough, becomes normal. At least I could walk the streets of Damascus, as many people did, despite the fact that danger was never far away.

In Beirut, I couldn't do that: I had become too famous. It was impossible for me to leave the hotel and walk without being mobbed by groups of young women who surrounded me, tormented me with all sorts of questions, touched and grabbed at me. But in Damascus, I was at ease; fame took a different form—I had become a source of pride for my people. When people recognized me, they would smile and nod; we would exchange a few words at most. I was from this area; my taking part in the show was also theirs, as was my elimination, so obviously political, which was clear to everyone. Perhaps it was respect, perhaps shyness, or perhaps it was as if they already knew me and therefore didn't feel the need to make a big thing of meeting me on the street.

As I had to take a year off from my education at the institute in order to participate in the television show, I had to wait a while before the next academic year started. While I waited, I decided to work as a dancer, choreographer, and teacher. I was paid more as a dancer than before, and I was teaching at three dance schools. With the extra money, I could afford an English course. I also moved to a safer apartment in Al-Tadamon with my mother, brother, and sister. The new apartment was safer because it was on the ground floor, which would enable us to flee quickly if bombs should fall there.

There was a new development in my experience in teaching dance. As well as teaching at the three dance schools, I volunteered to teach dance to children with special challenges. One group had Down syndrome. I wanted to help them feel the presence of their bodies. When I saw them dancing, and happy, my heart was full of joy because I had put a smile on their faces. I also taught a group of children at SOS Children's Villages, many of whom had been orphaned because of the war. I was able to establish a connection with these kids on a personal level; I could feel their need to feel safe, happy, and understood. So I supported them by giving them the most precious thing I have: *dance*. I wanted them to dance, dream, and forget and overcome what they had experienced in the war.

I WAS WITH SAEED on a bus full of people in Damascus, heading for the studio of a local radio station that had asked me for an interview. A woman was staring at me and smiling; she must have recognized me.

"Have you seen that woman? I think she's looking at you."

"Yes, I noticed."

"Does it annoy you?"

"No, not at all. There's nothing bad in it."

Saeed was always worried about people recognizing me. On the one hand, he knew how annoying it had been for me in Beirut, though it was different here; and on the other, I sensed that he felt a bit protective of me. Also, you never knew whom you might come across. I had had threats before; but now, I got worrying phone calls and messages with horrendous threats every other day.

Being popular had brought this into my life: I became a symbol for those who fight in the name of freedom and thus a symbol to be destroyed by those who wanted to deny that freedom. I was the physical, living incarnation of what they hated most, the antithesis of their credo. "We will cut your mother into pieces," "We will find your sister and rape her," "We will shoot you in the legs as punishment because you're too stubborn to die." But the most common threat was to decapitate me and hang my head at the entrance to Al-Yarmouk as a lesson to the other inhabitants.

I learned over time to let them pass, to pay no heed, to hang up the phone and tell myself that if they really wanted to take me out, they'd have done it already. All they really wanted was to scare me, and I wouldn't give them that satisfaction. And yet, I wasn't completely inured to them. And I still am not. I carry my life on my neck. "Dance or Die"—my tattoo—is the driving force that keeps me going. I live the way I want or I die.

"You knew that in the end, fame would lead to this sort of problem," Saeed said.

Saeed knew perfectly well what I was thinking about, and why. He was the only one who knew about it, besides the police, who were still preoccupied with bigger matters.

"I don't know precisely how many people have seen you dance on television, but there must be millions. I wonder what they all thought of you."

He stared out of the window as the bus bounced over potholes, and I held on to him so I wouldn't fall. As if suddenly remembering something, he asked, "But have you heard anything from your father since you got back? Has he called you?"

No. He hadn't called, but up to then, I hadn't even thought about my father. I looked out of the bus window, and another question came to mind: "Had my father ever seen me dance?"

AS THE YEARS OF THE war passed, the factions controlling Al-Yarmouk changed, and the people changed too. Some escaped; others resigned themselves to living in that hell, out on the streets, in a way they would never have imagined they had the courage to do. My family changed. Three of my uncles were killed in the fighting. It was impossible to say who killed them, just as two of my cousins had died in mysterious circumstances. Each time a family member died, we wondered, "Who is next?"

People who find themselves with their lives in danger and yet survive carry forever the scars of the experience. For example, for months my brother would wake up every night shouting, "Not my hands, don't break my hands, I want to continue to play musical instruments." And after that, he suddenly became really quiet, the complete opposite of the cheerful extrovert he had always been. As for my sister, her beauty and independence proved to be a curse for her. I got through it all better than either of them because I always behaved as though I was on stage, hiding certain feelings, acting out others, and venting what I suppressed through my dancing. In any case, we all, without exception, lost something of ourselves in every single challenge we had to face, with the constant fear of losing all feeling about life. Life, in our eyes, was slowly fading away.

And then there were those who managed to escape, like my father. He left Syria to join his wife, who was seeking refuge in Germany with their two daughters, my half-sisters. Like many others, they crossed the sea illegally, risking their lives in the hope of a better future.

The city itself had changed, of course, with many buildings gone, piles of rubble that no one had any intention of clearing. Memories and relics were the few things that remained. Sheets of cloth hung between one building and another, put there to block the view of snipers and to let people stretch their legs on the street and perhaps do a bit of shopping. Food cost ten times more than it did before the war, so people arranged to buy food and eat with their neighbors and friends; they felt fuller thanks to the sensation that comes with sharing. Those who could do so commuted to the center of Damascus, leaving in the morning and returning in the evening, and their working days were more peaceful because the center of Damascus was not at war, or at least not like the war we had in Al-Yarmouk. This helped them find the strength to keep going, like a breath of fresh air.

When the new academic year started, I returned to the institute. It gave me a reason to leave Al-Tadamon at least five days out of every seven, and from the moment I arrived, I would forget what I'd left behind. I used my bicycle to get there, as I preferred to use what little money I had to buy a sandwich at the institute rather than pay for public transport. Riding the bike also meant that I could warm up before classes. Above all, using the bike enabled me to avoid many checkpoints scattered throughout the neighborhood and the neighborhood just to the north, Al-Midan, which I also had to cross to reach the center of Damascus. There were twelve checkpoints I had to go through. Every day, with each checkpoint I passed, a chapter of my life passed through my mind.

One day, I approached one of these checkpoints without concern. It wasn't dangerous looking, and usually the soldiers would simply ask me what I did and where I was going. When I told them I studied dance, they often laughed and asked me to prove it. There were two possibilities at that point—one was that I could show them my student card from the institute, which was usually enough to get me through. The other was that they might ask me to dance for them.

This time, the soldiers had been ordering the men passing through the checkpoint to line up with their backs to the wall. As I approached, a soldier gestured to me to do the same thing. It would be pointless trying to speak to him; I just did what I was told and hoped the delay wouldn't make me late for class. I took up the position he indicated and waited in silence for a good ten minutes. A general got out of a jeep and started inspecting us, one by one, staring into our eyes. When he came to me, he stopped and said, "I know you; your face is familiar."

"Perhaps it's because I live around here and I take this road every day," I said, calmly and submissively.

"No, no . . . I remember you from something else. Are you the dancer?"

I was taken aback. I was frightened. "Will he arrest me?" I thought. Usually I was the one to identify myself as "the dancer." Had he already stopped me and remembered the good laugh he had at my expense? Whatever—it was pointless to lie.

"Yes, that's me."

"I've seen you on television," he said curtly. "Why are you here, you idiot?"

"I live here."

"Why have you returned? Why didn't you stay there? You were becoming famous, and you'd certainly have had a better life."

"I have to finish my studies."

"Ah. Your studies. Do you really need that? You know, I liked you on that program, even though I know nothing about dance. Every time you made it from one episode to the next, my men and I fired our guns into the air in celebration."

The simplicity of the man and his shining eyes touched me. I felt he had invested some hope in me, and seeing me again, here, felt like a defeat for him.

"Thank you. But now, if you want to help me, I have a dance class that begins in a few minutes, and if you keep me here . . . "

"Right, right."

The general stood to one side and ordered a soldier to bring me my bicycle, which I'd left just a few yards before the checkpoint. I got on the bike and turned to say good-bye. But he came over to me and, pointing discreetly at the line of men behind him, said in a low voice, "Listen. Don't imagine that we enjoy doing this sort of thing—we're ordered to do it and we have no choice. As soon as you can, get out of this country—it's no place for you."

"I wish I could. I will try, as soon as I complete my studies."

I set off again for the institute, happy that I wouldn't be late, happy too that this time it had worked out this way. The general seemed to be a reasonable person. It all depended on who was there in front of you, and that was what drove me mad—you might die or survive, at the discretion of a man like you. It was impossible to keep control over these people—they armed them too quickly, without even preparing them beforehand. These are men who might have lost everything, might be blind in their desperation and ready to kill anything that moved, just to vent their rage. Every family in Syria had lost someone. Then again, the worst thing I'd ever seen were those patrolling the streets under the influence of drugs or alcohol—full of stuff that made them hallucinate and gave them the false courage to dance through the bullets, suppressing every iota of their humanity to the point where they were capable of shooting a child just for kicks. I was thinking: "The war has destroyed our history and our present. By saving our children we save our future, but who will protect the children? Artists have the same duty as soldiers: to fight for their country. A country without culture and art is not a country worth fighting for."

I chased these thoughts away. Getting through the checkpoint was the moment when I left Al-Yarmouk, Al-Tadamon, and all their horrors behind me. It was the moment when I felt good, free of the worries and memories that in any case would be back with me that evening—hoping always that my return journey would be as smooth as the journey coming here in the morning. I stood up and pedaled as fast as I could to get to class.

I WAS BIKING TOWARD the institute early one morning, the first feeble rays of light warming my face. Around me the landscape was in shreds, and I thought about how different life had been in a time so far away, it felt as though it never actually existed. But slipping through the ruins on my bike, silent and fast, made the atmosphere more bearable, creating a sensation of detachment from all this destruction. I felt that as long as I was pedaling, no bullet would find me, no building would collapse on me. And I was careful to avoid the shards of glass on the ground—a punctured tire would be a real problem.

I passed through the Al-Midan neighborhood, smiling at the young people walking timidly through the grounds of the Al-Hassan Mosque and thinking of my studies—just a few months more and I would be finished. I felt both glad and sad about this. I would miss the institute, studying all those different subjects: under the four-year program that would take me six years to complete, I'd studied modern, jazz, classical, neoclassical, and contemporary dance; pantomime; acting; stage design; and lighting. Suddenly, a terrible thought came to me, something I hadn't yet considered: once I'd completed my studies, I might be called up to join the army.

I braked suddenly. The army. This was crazy. No way, never. I could never kill anyone, never harm anyone. And for whose cause, anyway?

What awful thoughts, cropping up at a rare peaceful moment. I told myself that in any case, there was still time—four months— before I would graduate. I got back on my bike and forced myself to think of other things. I listened to the birds singing undaunted, despite everything. I lifted my face toward the sky to gather as much light as possible—it was still weak, fragile, and precious, as though it might disappear from one moment to the next. The breeze stirred the leaves on the few spindly trees, a sweet sound for those who know how to listen for it.

"BEEP-BEEP!"

A car behind me hit its horn and braked violently to avoid running me over.

"What the hell are you doing? Get out of here!" the driver shouted at me as he passed.

I didn't understand. I moved quickly to the edge of the road and stopped, leaning against the guardrail. But there were no guardrails on the route I took every morning. Or speeding cars with agitated drivers. No one shouted, no one blasted their horn. What was happening?

I squeezed my eyes shut and opened them again, trying to assure myself that I wasn't dreaming. No, ahead of me lay a four-lane highway—I was on the freeway with my bicycle, even though a few seconds ago I had been traveling along the roads of Al-Midan, stirring up clouds of dust. How did I get here? I didn't know if someone brought me here or I came of my own accord. I had a headache that was getting stronger, throbbing behind my forehead. It was as if my brain were trying to split open my skull to force its way out. I was on the freeway with my bicycle, the cars rushing by, their passengers looking at me in astonishment. They must have thought I was mad, because now I moved forward, leaning on the guardrail, the bicycle in my left hand, my right hand cradling my forehead, keeping it from splitting open. I staggered. I was going to throw up. I had to get out of there. I had to get to class.

By the following month, things were better, much better. The painkillers had started working without me realizing it, and I could clearly feel my brain relaxing, settling within my head, which lay on a soft pillow. I had another pillow under my knees.

On my twenty-sixth birthday, I went to a hospital in Damascus to get a magnetic resonance imaging (MRI) scan of my brain. Because of my migraines, my doctor had advised me to have the scan, which up to then I had refused. But after what happened on the highway, my mother insisted that I should follow my doctor's advice.

I hadn't wanted to spend this day in this way. For years, I'd avoided having any serious tests done because my migraines had never really been serious. Painful, sure, or else they wouldn't have been real migraines. The headaches started when the war broke out, so I figured that my symptoms were psychosomatic. And I had so much to sort through during that time that dealing with my headaches on top of everything would have been too much.

But this time, it was different. This time, I really had reason to worry. Finding myself on the freeway like that, out of the blue, without even remembering how I got there; not knowing how long I had lost consciousness. That's what really frightened me as I lay in the hospital bed. They were ready to put me into a threatening-looking machine—a long, white cylinder with a mouth ready to swallow me up. The doctors wanted to look inside my head. I told them not to root around in the depths too much, but they didn't laugh.

True, I'd already seen other doctors about this migraine problem. Blood pressure was the most common diagnosis—some advice on reducing stress, a couple of painkillers that didn't always work, and then straight home until the next migraine. But I couldn't really blame them, since I was the one who was so blasé. I'd already spent enough time in the hospital, and I had no intention of dedicating any more time to it. I no longer wanted to have anything to do with white coats, rubber gloves, fluorescent light on the ceiling, mysterious bags of fluid hanging above me, little tubes under my skin, masks, and those paper slippers covering visitors' shoes. But here I was.

The bed started moving slowly, taking me into the jaws of the machine. It was like a coffin. Really clean and smooth, but still a coffin. I was in no way calm; hospitals were risky places in my experience—there was always a contraindication, a side effect, the chance that something might go wrong. Proof of this was the fact that they all left the room! Just before my body was completely enveloped by the big tube, I took another quick look around me: I was completely alone, with no one waiting for me in the corridor on the other side of the glass. Not even my mother, even though I knew she would have come with me willingly. But I didn't ask her, as I didn't want her to see me in these moments of weakness.

The bed stopped moving, the cylinder rotated, a blinding light came on. I closed my eyes tightly as I'd been told to do. I searched through my memories for a reminiscence that might keep me company, make the time pass more quickly.

It was another birthday, and I was spending it with my first girlfriend. I must have been fifteen; she was five years older. She wrote and read a lot and was really perceptive about people and their inner thoughts. She never judged anyone and supported me in my passion for dancing more than anyone else, except my mother. She spurred me on to express myself in ways that were new to me, pushing me to write to free my thoughts in the form of words, putting down on paper the creations of my imagination, which at the time were extremely vivid. I saw the world around me in a different way, through dreamlike visions, associating the people of my life with figures taken from the natural world. She used to describe me in her writings as "the king of beginnings" or "the temple dancer," and I described her as "my diamond." The memory of my first love led to the next thought. "Where did those stories I wrote end up? Of course . . . destroyed with the rest of the house."

The bed started moving again, sliding silently out of the tunnel. I touched my face, my head . . . everything seemed to be fine, everything in the same place as before. The doors opened with a noise like something from a science fiction film, increasing my feelings of unease. I got up and walked toward the exit, and a light came on to my right, illuminating a room that only now was visible behind a pane of glass. Inside was a small group of doctors conferring in a serious and concentrated manner behind a computer screen. I could just make out an image of my brain on the screen. It was so strange to see it like this, in sections. But there was a detail in the image that I was pretty sure shouldn't be there.

"How did it go?" a man in a white coat suddenly asked me. I'd almost bumped into him, so lost was I in my thoughts.

"How do you think it went?"

"Fine, fine. We'll call you as soon as the results are ready."

"Thank you, Doctor."

I headed quickly toward the stairs. I had to get out of this place as soon as possible.

"Ahmad!" he shouted to me. "Make sure you bring a parent with you next time."

A week later, I was back in the hospital with my mother. I stared at the wall, my arms crossed, waiting for the doctor to arrive. My mother nervously drummed her fingers on her knees. As for me, I was not the least bit nervous. Ever since I saw that sinister thing in my head, I'd been trying to imagine what it might be, but now I'd abandoned the exercise. I might as well not think about it, because before long they would tell us. I had not said anything about it to my mother.

During the week, I'd been thinking about the stories I wrote as a teenager that had come back to me during the MRI. A lot of details had come back to me. In one story, I wrote about a vision of mine: "I saw my mother as a tree with a wide trunk, high and solid with firm roots that went off in all directions, and long branches that reached up toward the sky and from which spread an infinity of leaves, flowers, and fruits. My many uncles and aunts and cousins were instead butterflies that flew around me, all of them in different colors. I saw myself inside the belly of a whale, and I was trying to get out, holding a rope and climbing upward toward the light. But once I was out of the whale, the butterflies transformed into creepy-looking bats that flew into me and tugged at my hair. There was only one butterfly that could lead me away from them, a blue butterfly that symbolized my heart."

"Here we are, if you'd like to follow me to my office."

The moment of truth had arrived. We walked along the corridor behind the doctor, a man of fifty or so, with that look of a person who knows more than anyone else, his steps decided and proud, his bearing almost invincible in his white coat. He had us sit down in front of him, his desk separating us and reminding us of who was healthy and who ill.

"I have the MRI results here. It's something quite serious, but don't be alarmed because even though we're a bit late in diagnosing it, it is curable. First of all, how do you feel, Ahmad? Have you had any more attacks?"

"No, no, nothing at all since last week."

"Excellent."

"Doctor, I never had an attack as strong as that last one. I always thought they were just stress-related headaches; that's what other doctors always told me."

"Well. . . we really have reached a point now where we have to do something about it. We see from the images that you have a brain edema, Ahmad."

My mother and I looked at each other as though he was speaking another language. What did that mean?

"To put it in layman's terms," he continued, "you have a bubble of liquid in your brain. These are the scans . . . look."

He showed us freshly printed images. They were the images I'd caught a glimpse of a week ago, but now I could see them much more clearly. The four scans of the quarters of my skull looked like four perfect walnuts cut in half—or rather, they would have been perfect if it weren't for one little detail standing out: a white mark, round but not perfectly circular, relatively small. Seen like this, the bubble seemed innocuous.

"And is it comfortable in there?" I asked.

"I advise you not to joke about this, Ahmad. It's an urgent condition that can easily become critical in a very short space of time. That last attack you had was a warning sign."

"And so, what do we do now?" my mother said; she was perhaps the most worried person in the room.

"An operation."

"What? Open up my head?"

"Exactly, to get the bubble out. It's a delicate operation, which involves its own risks, but we've done them before."

"No way. You're not opening up my head."

"Ahmad," my mother said, "listen to the doctor."

"You've already experienced some of the consequences. Ahmad, it's a serious situation—you must face up to it."

He looked me straight in the eye, while my mother hid her eyes behind her hand. I'd made my decision, and his big words weren't going to make me change my mind. For all I knew, I might walk out of here, step on a mine, and be blown to bits; or I might find myself in front of a car full of explosives and be splattered all over a wall.

"If I have to die, I will die while dancing, or on top of a mountain, but not on the operating table."

They both looked at me as though I were crazy. They spent the next hour trying to convince me—pleading with me and then shouting at me. They called me a madman, reckless, selfish; but my ears were closed to them.

Instead, I thought of the ending of the story I wrote as a teenager: "My father appeared. He was a scorpion: black as night, with two large, sharp claws and that stinger, always held on high, ready to attack. He enjoyed frightening me and hurting me, running between my legs, climbing up my back, nipping me and stinging me, but without ever injecting enough poison to kill me."

And I knew now, as a man, that that poison really did exist. It was actually inside me and had been inside me all this time, accumulating in the most sheltered and least obvious corner of my body. I took the images in my hand again—there it was, compressed between my skull and my brain, a little bubble of white poison.

FOR YEARS, I HAD challenged death without ever losing, and at the same time I'd done things I'd never have imagined possible. Yet with each goal I reached, my sense of victory, of achievement was torn from me. I was always on a knife's edge. Just like the precipice I was walking along now. The cliff I was on was very high, seen from up here, but what difference would it have made if it were low? I seemed to have lost control of my life; my will did not count for much. And if I fell from that cliff and died, so what? I had to die sometime. Maybe the army would knock on my door and make me wear a uniform. Or it might be this bubble in my head that killed me. Or a sniper might shoot me in the head, now that I was so visible.

The qualification I was studying for wouldn't save me from my destiny. The will to dance had pulled me out of a few dangerous situations, but at what cost? My family's hatred for me; my parents' separation; that little brother who was never born; the threats from the fanatics.

Should my foot slip at the edge of that cliff, should I nearly fall as the stone beneath me crumbled, I would watch the broken pieces tumble down for what would seem an infinity, with no noise as they touched the ground. It wasn't that I felt invincible; it's that I felt in no control of decisions about my life—anything I did would always be turned and manipulated in a logic that was the opposite of my will. So why bother making the effort?

Soon after that visit to the doctor, an idea began to take shape in my head. Soon it reached the point where it became a certainty: if making any effort was pointless, if I couldn't react to external, unpredictable forces, then I might as well just play along with them.

I knew exactly what I was going to do. I asked my sister, Rawan, to hold my cell phone so that she could make the lens take in the entire width of the rooftop—I was in the frame, with the minaret behind me and the clean, intense blue of the sky around me. I got undressed, leaving just my dance shorts on.

"Let's see if I die now."

Rawan filmed me. I took up a position at the center of the frame, and with no music, in the unnatural silence of the hours of truce in the fighting, I started dancing. I moved freely, in the way that I wanted everyone to be able to do. I was sure that if all soldiers took dance classes, they wouldn't get so much pleasure out of killing each other. Nor out of killing civilians.

"Let's see if I die now," I said to myself, as I openly challenged the forces that sought to hinder me. Kill me now, immediately, I challenged, because if I continued to live, then I would publish this video on the internet, reach people all over the world who would understand me, love me for what I was.

I accepted that if I could not live for myself, I could live for others. I could make sure that my battles were for a purpose greater than my simple personal satisfaction. My only weapon would be dance.

In the description of the video, I wrote:

Dance has no borders. Dance needs no passports. Dance knows no nationality. Dance is humanity.

The video worked: in no time, I had hundreds of views on YouTube—not a lot compared to some crazy figures, but in my own little world, the number symbolized something much greater. For people to dedicate a bit of their spare time to watching a stranger dance on the internet, one of many, was a success in itself. If they then managed to understand the message I was trying to convey, then it would be a total success.

I was not in search of fame—that was part of the *So You Think You Can Dance* experience, and having experienced fame, I knew just how noxious it could be. No, all I wanted to do was something small. I didn't believe in armies and weapons, but I couldn't just complain and do nothing; I had to act. Act in my own way, obviously, and those few views on the internet created the recognition that I was looking for; they meant that I was heading in the right direction. When it came to it, I wanted to exit the stage knowing I'd left something good behind me.

The power of the internet. For those of us who lived in those wastelands, where everything was so far away and difficult to reach, opening up computer screens projected us into an almost magical dimension. We saw the wonders of the West, the latest fashions, innovative artists, the rest of the world discussing our war . . . even though the war coverage made me laugh, as a computer screen couldn't possibly convey a full sense of what we were living through, just as we couldn't fully understand most of what reached us from Europe or the United States.

But the greatest impact that the web had on my life concerned dance. Perhaps if there had been no internet, things would have gone differently. Since I was a teenager, I spent hours on YouTube watching and admiring videos of shows, rehearsals, lessons, and interviews with talented and celebrated dancers. I used to show them to my cousins, explaining every step, every movement, together with the stories of the ballets. Then my father would come along and make us switch everything off.

One dancer in particular attracted my attention more than any other: Roberto Bolle, the *primo ballerino* of La Scala of Milan. He always conveyed to me a sense of perfection, not only as a dancer but as a person. He was discreet, intelligent, committed to humanitarian causes, and above all humble, a quality rare in the world of dance. Watching him, more than anyone else, I found much of the energy that kept me going because Bolle made me dream (as he does now, as I write these words). He was, and continues to be, my total role model—I'd like to be like him one day.

As I watched the rooftop video I made, I could forget that I was ill and threatened by extremists, and that in a month's time I would graduate and could be conscripted. Why should I have stopped myself being happy, at least in a world that didn't exist?

My cell phone rang—an unknown number. Some fundamentalist again? I decided to see what they wanted.

"Ahmad Joudeh?" a woman's voice asked. Well, it wasn't extremists—extremists would never allow a woman to represent them.

"Yes. It's me."

"You received a friend request on Facebook a few days ago . . . we need you to accept it."

"Sorry? Who are you? How did you get my number? And how do you know about my Facebook?"

"That's irrelevant. I can tell you I'm calling on behalf of the government. Now, it's important that you accept this friend request. It's a Dutch journalist who'd like to work with you."

"Do you have any idea how many requests and messages full of insults I receive every day? Who is this journalist? And why are you so concerned as to call me up on the phone?"

"I don't know who it is, or what they want. My job is simply to make sure to put you in contact with him. I imagine it must be something important, if they've mobilized so many people just for this."

"But how do I know all this is true?"

"Listen, I haven't got all day. Accept the request and see how it goes. Trust me, do as I say. Good-bye."

She hung up without leaving me any time to respond. The call left me in a funk. At this rate, I was heading for paranoia. But the woman had seemed genuine; her voice wasn't nasty but solid, stable.

I went onto Facebook. There were a few friend requests awaiting confirmation, but I had stopped paying attention to them. I scrolled through, searching for something imprecise—a clue, a detail. Of course, that woman could have at least told me the journalist's name. But suddenly, there it was—a name that stood out from the others. It had to be him; it was the only name that didn't sound Arabic—Roozbeh Kaboly. Perhaps the woman was right; it made sense for me to at least see what it was about. I had one foot in the grave already, and things couldn't get any worse. I accepted the request.

I leaned back in the chair, staring for a few minutes at the computer screen. Nothing happened. I let myself be transported by my imagination. The reality was that this was the end of my life, so my imagination could only be a beginning.

A burst of machine-gun fire arrived on the wind and woke me abruptly. The fighting was starting again. I closed the shutters, barricaded myself at home, hidden as always between those walls, which were covered by newspapers, behind this screen. I clicked on another video of Bolle dancing, headphones on and volume at maximum, leaving the Facebook tab open on one side, waiting for something to happen. Anything, anything to escape this moment.

NINE

IN THE SUMMER OF 2016, a new chapter in my life began to unfold . . . via Facebook:

Roozbeh Kaboly:

Hello Ahmad.

My name is Roozbeh Kaboly. I'm a war reporter, a journalist with Dutch national television.

I have been working in and on Syria a lot.

I'm writing to you because I found out about you thanks to your videos on Facebook and YouTube— I saw them while doing some research on dance in Syria. I must tell you I was really struck by your story, by you as a person and by the message that you seek to convey.

My job involves telling stories. If you like the idea, I would like to make a reportage about you and tell your story in our television news program.

Ahmad Joudeh:

Hello Roozbeh.

Yes, I'd been told that you wanted to film me, but no one has explained any details.

Can you tell me more, please?

Roozbeh Kaboly:

Hello Ahmad.

First of all, thanks for the reply.

I'm a filmmaker. I make videos.

I think that filming the places where you live, the people in your life, everyday reality basically, might be a good way of telling your wonderful story. Perhaps in a new rough and ready way, just as I do when I'm doing war reportage. But without neglecting the dancing, obviously, which is a fundamental element in your story.

I live in Amsterdam, but don't worry about that—I come to Syria regularly as a war reporter. And I will try to come to Damascus soon to meet you. If I manage that, would you agree with me filming you?

Ahmad Joudeh:

OK. For me that's fine.

I'd never ask you to come to Syria because it's dangerous now. But if we were to meet up here, of course I would work with you.

But can I ask you why you really want to work with me?

So . . . when do you want to come? And how much time will the filming take?

I don't have much left.

Roozbeh Kaboly:

Perfect.

I've chosen you because I get the impression from your photographs and videos that you're a truly professional dancer. And then I discovered that you've already worked on television, so you must have experience of working in front of the camera.

And then, I'm simply really interested in getting to know you.

You won't need to worry about any of the details—I can get permits to film wherever I want and it won't be my first time working in the Middle East and in Syria. And obviously I won't do anything that'll put you in danger.

Why don't you have much time? In that case I can come even immediately.

Ahmad Joudeh:

Because I've almost finished my studies, and any time now I might be conscripted and then I'll have to forget about dancing, and probably my family too. That's if I survive.

Roozbeh Kaboly:

OK Ahmad. I'll get the journey organized and I'll do everything to get a visa as soon as possible.
I'll let you know when I'm arriving, but it'll take a bit of time, perhaps a month, perhaps two . . . I don't know.

In the meantime, thanks for your help.

Inshallah, I hope it works out and that we do a good job. We shall see . . .

Yalla, all best

IN JULY, I COMPLETED my studies by performing my graduation dance project before an audience that included Syria's minister of culture. I was the only student who graduated that year from the dance department, and I was filled with a strange feeling of happiness mixed with fear about the future.

I continued choreographing for a dance company in Damascus, where I was a ballet master. One morning, as I was teaching, I felt my phone vibrating in my pocket.

"Excuse me, guys, but I have to go out for two minutes," I said. "Take a break in the meantime. Do a bit of stretching."

As I left the room, the dancers sighed, exhausted, and flopped to the floor. The summer heat didn't help; perhaps it was time to call it a day. But first of all, I wanted to see who was calling.

"Hello, Ahmad."

It was him. The only person I knew with that accent.

"Roozbeh! How are you?"

"I'm fine, fine, and you? I'm in a restaurant now, in Old Damascus. I'll text you the address in a minute."

"OK, sure. I understand, but let me finish my work first. That will take about an hour, and then it'll take me half an hour on my bike."

"All right, an hour and a half. See you soon, Ahmad."

He was now in town, and it looked as though everything we'd spoken about was really going to happen.

"Guys . . . I realize you're all really tired; we all are, just as we're all struggling with the heat. So, come on, back on your feet and let's start the choreography where we left off."

"YOU'RE TALLER THAN I thought you would be." Roozbeh held out his hand. He was shorter than me—fair skin, pale. "It's a pleasure to meet you finally, Ahmad."

"The pleasure's mine."

I shook his hand, gripping it tightly. I wasn't sure who he was. A journalist from Holland, that's all I knew.

He pointed to the table in the café, indicating where we should take our seats. A woman was sitting there already.

"And she is . . . ?" I asked him.

"She is the translator and fixer."

We approached the table and the woman extended her hand.

"Pleased to meet you. I'm Emma," she said in a firm voice that sounded familiar.

"My pleasure. But have we met before?"

"No . . . or rather, on the phone. I was the one who called you about Roozbeh."

"Nice to meet you."

After a moment's silence, Roozbeh said, "I am honored to meet you in person. For us, it's difficult to believe that someone like you really exists. Doing what you do, keeping going despite everything, in this place, in these conditions."

"Thank you. I just do what I love to do. Dance is rooted in my soul. I couldn't do otherwise."

"Please tell me about yourself," he said. "What do you get up to during your typical day? My head's full of ideas."

We spent a good hour or so talking about daily life in Damascus and the surroundings, and about my dance activities—performances with Enana and other companies; the shows I was leading; my choreographies at Damascus Opera House and other theaters; and the dance classes I was conducting, including my support of challenged children. I told him about my education at the Higher Institute for Dramatic Arts and the likelihood that I'd soon be joining the army. He listened carefully, interrupting only to ask precise questions, and he responded to my stories with signs of interest and curiosity. He really did seem excited about the idea of working with me.

"It's all really interesting, Ahmad. I want to document everything. Your story is incredible and really has to be told. When do you think we can start?"

"Tomorrow if you like."

"Great! Tell me where you'd like me to film you dancing. Where do you want to dance?"

Everything in my head stopped. I wasn't expecting this question. I'd never even thought about it on my own. Where would I like to dance? I'd already done it on the roof, and I'd even filmed it. While I twiddled my thumbs, as though they might magically come up with the answer I was looking for, it came to me, clear as a bell:

"In Al-Yarmouk."

"Wouldn't that be dangerous?"

"Al-Yarmouk, out in the street."

"But, but the neighborhood's closed. There are checkpoints everywhere; how could we do that?"

I looked into his eyes. I knew what I was saying, I knew what I wanted, I knew it could be dangerous . . . but I couldn't help it.

"If you're really asking me where I want to dance, my answer is on the streets of Al-Yarmouk. And you did say getting permits wasn't a problem, no?"

"Perhaps you're right. We might as well go all the way, no? And show people what your life really consists of. Do you think we can get a permit to film in the neighborhood?" he asked

Emma, who'd been listening attentively. She thought for a moment and nodded.

"Yes, I should be able to manage that. When do you need it for?"

I looked at Roozbeh. From what I saw in his eyes, he seemed to trust me completely. He wanted me to take the lead from here.

"For tomorrow," I said with determination.

"OK," she said. "Excuse me a moment then. I have to make a couple of calls."

She went outside. Roozbeh and I were left in silence, each absorbed in his own thoughts, each worried about tomorrow. I didn't know what to expect—I hadn't set foot in Al-Yarmouk for a long time. I was scared of what I would see there more than whatever danger we would face.

Music awoke us from our reverie. At a table not far from us, a birthday was being celebrated. I'd already noticed them—people laughing and shouting happily, but now standing and taking one another's hands.

People were getting ready to dance the dabka, as Syrians do when we celebrate. The men started dancing around the restaurant, moving with agility between the tables, dodging the waiters, involving anyone who looked eager to join in.

When the long line passed next to us, I got up.

"Shall we?" I said.

He might have thought I meant that we should leave the restaurant, but instead I joined the back of the dance line, taking the hand of the last person. I held out my free hand to Roozbeh, and he happily accepted the invitation; then he invited Emma, so she took his hand. We all danced together.

It occurred to me, how strange it was that meeting certain people and being involved in certain events can happen so naturally, so unexpectedly. These were moments, I realized, that had to be accepted. They were too precious to let slip through our hands, and we never can know where they may take us.

Roozbeh surprised me. We danced quickly from one side of the restaurant to the other. He was laughing. "We might as well laugh now," I said, "because today is today. Tomorrow, we will see."

THE NEXT MORNING my mother made breakfast, which we ate in a sort of sacred silence, one of those silences that precede important events. The tension was very high; you could almost feel it if you moved your hand through the air.

Emma had told Roozbeh that we should wait at the checkpoint on the border of Al-Yarmouk. Someone would come with the permit for entering the neighborhood and for filming, and they would also escort us through the neighborhood's dangerous streets. Evidently, the presence of a television camera from Europe helped on such occasions.

The heat made the wait almost unbearable, but soon our patience was rewarded—not one person, as we'd imagined, but several soldiers appeared, marching toward us, armed to the teeth, their expressions tough and determined. They marched confidently straight at us, which made us a little scared. When they were close enough, I saw that they were murmuring to one another, some smiling and some shaking their heads as though saying "No."

There was no time for formalities.

"So you're the people who have to be escorted in there?" an officer asked, his finger pointing up the long, straight road into Al-Yarmouk.

"That's us," Emma said, trying to soften them a bit.

"Very well. We have the permit, and we'll keep hold of it. If you're ready, I suggest we move immediately. We'll walk in single file, with all of you in the middle. Careful where you put your feet because there might be mines."

I thought about the poor guy at the front of the line, and I couldn't stop myself from saying, "I'll take the lead!"

The soldiers looked at me as though I were mad.

"I'm from this place, I lived here in this neighborhood, and I used to go along this road every day. You're all safer if you're behind me."

The leader grunted and nodded.

We set off. I walked briskly, head high—unafraid of stepping on a mine, unafraid of being shot at, and above all unafraid of being in the streets of the neighborhood of my origins.

"Where are we going exactly?" Roozbeh asked while filming.

"Home," I said instinctively. "Where is my home?" I was unsure. I saw only rubble. The war had left only destruction. Every life had disappeared.

I looked into Roozbeh's eyes. He hesitated a second or two before nodding, but the reaction of the rest of our escort was different—there was an indistinct, general buzz of complaint, but it seemed as though we were in charge. Thanks to the presence of that television camera.

Only one voice came to me distinctly.

"And to think that we're all here risking our lives so that he can dance!"

I could have turned around and explained the importance of what we were doing—much more important than shooting at enemies. I could even have retreated and let one of the soldiers lead the rest of us. But I was driven by something else: in the heart of my neighborhood, a new Al-Yarmouk was revealing itself to me in all its horror, and I suddenly felt my strength disappear. Memories flashed before my eyes, as clearly as if they were recent events, and as though they were there to try to repair the irreparable. Abd and his wife and their kids had lived over there, where there was now nothing left but a few pillars of concrete; no trace of the life of the past and of those who lived, laughed, cried in that building. There was the workshop where I used to go to work on my bicycle—all that was left was a buckled metal shutter. This sight broke my heart. On the other side was blackness as deep as the night. Or as deep as death. I could walk into that workshop with my eyes closed without bumping into anything, so well did I remember the space, the distance between the walls, where all the tools had been. Whenever I worked on my bike, the owner shouted at me, telling me to put the tools back where I found them.

My foot touched something that rolled into the road, causing a little stir among our group—a plastic doll's head, its hair all burned and its wide-open green eyes staring at us. It seemed to be trying to say something to us. It was smiling, but I thought it was asking for help.

I wished I could cry. It was all too much. I hadn't expected the day to work out like this. But I should have known, instead of throwing myself blindly into something bigger than my capacity for bearing all this. But it was too late; at this point, I had to go all the way.

"Halt!" the leader shouted. "Behind that curtain, ISIS is there," he said, pointing to a small side street, interrupted some twenty yards in by a small wall of bags of cement and some sheets hung between one building and another, to obstruct the snipers' view.

I searched again for Roozbeh's eyes. He'd been silent, busily taking in everything around him. From his expression, I understood that he didn't need any translation. He nodded. He knew the risks; he knew what was behind the makeshift curtain without my having to explain.

We started off again. I set myself up in front of the little wall, Roozbeh standing in front of me with the camera on his shoulder—nothing to protect us from whatever was there, except for my spirit. An unreal silence filled the air, as though everything had stopped, as though each grain of sand on the ground was asking what was about to happen. The silence had become unbearable.

Roozbeh started asking me questions. While I was answering, a single shot rang out. A cloud of dust rose just a few yards from me when another shot exploded, and then another. Roozbeh and I, still standing in the middle, looked at each other, motionless. It all happened in the space of a few seconds, and we didn't have time to realize what was happening. Roozbeh was still filming, and I continued with my answers. The soldiers looked up, trying to find out where the shots came from.

"Shall we take cover?" he shouted. I shook my head, refusing to abandon this opportunity to dance in Al-Yarmouk at that moment. He nodded.

I put my hands together in front of my chest. I felt my spirit entering my body, spreading its wings of fire from my back.

My soul is screaming
The time is coming
It's getting closer and closer
All the dreams are fading
All the colors are disappearing
My eyes are blinding
And my skin is tightening

The fire is losing its flames
It's cold around me
It's freezing inside me
My lord
Spare me from this suffering
Take my soul
And set an end for this pain
I am ready my lord.

I started moving my feet slowly, dragging them noisily. As often happens when I dance without music, I fell into a sort of trance—I closed my eyes, or perhaps I kept them open, but I no longer saw anything. I just let my body move freely, expressing itself in its own way. I let it free itself of the weight of terrestrial life, of the words full of meaning, of the tormenting images that surrounded me. I flew, free of all my chains, and for a minute or two I was elsewhere, forgetting the danger all around us.

Slowly, I came back to my senses; even more slowly, I recovered my breath. I was in shock, my limbs trembling. Dancing here meant everything to me, and at that precise moment I could feel that meaning right down to my bones. It was as though I could hear the souls of my late uncles and cousins all around me, and for a moment I was that child who used to play, carefree, in these streets. I also felt this would be the last time I would see Al-Yarmouk, given the big unknowns of my future. I danced as though it were the last dance of my life.

As soon as I returned to reality, I saw Roozbeh, still before me, in the same position as before, the camera still on his shoulder. Then I became aware of something else—the silence. Silence had fallen again on Al-Yarmouk. As soon as I started dancing, the firing behind the curtain stopped. The sniper could have shot me at any moment. The same question came to my mind that had come every time I faced death: Why?

Now that I had stopped moving, not even the wind was stirring. I looked at the soldiers, and they looked at me with curiosity, surprise, a sensitive expression on their faces that was out of place with the uniforms, the rifles heavy in their hands.

"Come . . . rest for a minute," a soldier said.

He was standing outside the alleyway, with a plastic chair in his hand. Who knows where he found it. This little gesture moved me, especially after their criticism. I didn't need to rest, but I wanted to acknowledge the gesture. As soon as I sat, he handed me some water. Another soldier came over to me.

"Look," he said, showing me his phone. "I videoed you while you were dancing. Do you want me to send it to you?"

We used Bluetooth so he could send me the video. I was even more moved—I'd touched the souls of soldiers, of people who build a fortress around their hearts in order to bear the horrors they have to live with every day. And it looked as though I also had had some effect on the sniper who was shooting at us. I felt like a winner!

As the composer Jonathan Larson said, "The opposite of war is not peace; it is creation." For me, to be able to create a piece of art in the middle of war was a blessing, which I will carry with me all my life.

"You know," the soldier who shot the video said, "you're doing something I've always dreamed of doing—being a dancer. But as you can see, it didn't work out for me." He lifted his rifle. "So, please, keep doing what you do. Do it for those of us who haven't managed."

"Have we finished here? Come on, let's march. Same formation as before, and the same route." The leader's grave and powerful voice thundered through the silent streets of the neighborhood, finding its way into every corner, into every crack in the shattered concrete, into every abandoned apartment.

On the way back, I continued looking behind me, taking a series of last looks at the neighborhood, trying to fix as many details as possible in my head. Perhaps I wasn't that bothered about returning here to see all this destruction. The destruction confirmed that if I meant to live, then I no longer belonged here, but what I really wanted was to return one day, to find it as it once was—free, full of life, with plenty of space to offer to anyone who needed it.

I saw the doll's head, waiting for someone to find what remained of its body.

"I DON'T WANT YOU going to these places on your own anymore, Ahmad."

Tears welled in my mother's eyes, though she was trying to hide it. The images of Al-Yarmouk that Roozbeh shot were playing before her, in all their devastating power. For her, too, it was terrible to see that what we once called our neighborhood was now nothing more than pieces of a jigsaw puzzle to be put back together. A jigsaw with many missing pieces to be filled, painfully, from memory.

In spite of the shock of seeing the video, she kept her head and gave us something to eat, as though everything were normal.

"And now, Ahmad," Roozbeh said between mouthfuls, "where do you want to dance tomorrow? And this time, don't risk getting us killed!"

He was making light of it, trying to make the atmosphere over dinner more relaxed.

"Palmyra. I want to dance in the Roman amphitheater."

I could see that Roozbeh knew what I wanted, knew the history of the place. He paused thoughtfully for a while, obviously considering the risks. My mother broke the silence.

"I'm coming with you this time."

This time the government didn't send soldiers to accompany us, but rather an army press officer. Including Roozbeh, my mother, Emma, and me, there were five of us, not counting the driver, in the car. A small expedition with a mission even riskier than that of the previous day—filming dancing in the amphitheater where ISIS in the past had organized mass executions. This time, there was even more at stake. My dancing was becoming a real challenge, a provocation.

The problems started at once. As soon as we reached the outskirts of Palmyra, we encountered a group of armed men blocking the road. They shouted at us in a language I didn't know—it certainly wasn't Arabic or English—and they gestured with their rifles for us to get out of the car.

Fear grabbed me by the throat, almost stopping my breath. I wasn't afraid for myself—I no longer had great expectations for my life—but I did fear for my mother. "If things start going wrong here, then the best-case scenario will be that they'll decapitate me in front of her," I thought. "That way, they would spare me from seeing harm done to my mother and the others."

As the men shouted and pointed their rifles at us, we looked at one another, with no clue what to do. The officer took a deep breath, opened the door, and got out, telling us to wait for him. We didn't move. We watched him walk a few yards from the car with some of the men, while the others stayed to guard us. We could see the officer talking and gesticulating in a back-and-forth exchange that lasted a long hour. In the meantime, the car languished out there in the sun, growing hotter and hotter. We were sweating with heat and tension. All sorts of images came to my mind, but all I wanted was to keep my mother safe.

Finally, he returned and announced victory. "They've given us permission to go through."

The mysterious men divided into two rows, leaving us just enough space to pass through. We drove slowly, and then suddenly accelerated as soon as we were out of the danger zone, heading for the administrative office.

In the office, which was where we had to go to get the filming permit, things couldn't have been different. Thanks to the presence of Roozbeh's camera—he always had it with him—we were welcomed politely. The staff offered us support of all kinds, and we soon had a permit for four hours' filming. No more than that.

We crossed through Palmyra, again on a road with ruins on both sides—another city that hadn't been spared by the war. This time, I was not panicking at the sight of ripped-up roads and gutted buildings, though I was affected. But my mother was very upset: this place had been her home, and she was processing her loss. She studied everything through the windows, her eyes darting from one memory to another, wringing her hands in her own desolation at seeing the destruction.

I should have stopped her from coming, even though she would have hated me for it. Seeing her like this was more painful than any harm I could ever inflict on myself, more painful than any physical or emotional torture. I no longer gave much thought to my own suffering; I no longer dwelled on it, and I had learned to live with it, but seeing my mother in this state was an unbearable burden. It was blurring my heart. I looked elsewhere, closed my eyes. She was everything I had, as I did not even have myself anymore. She was the thing that, now more than anything else, must be protected.

When we arrived at the theater, I was suddenly consumed by anger for the tragedy that had taken place there. I felt an irresistible need to do something, anything to bring all this to an end. I jumped onto the stage area, where dozens of men had been made to kneel in a line, each with a child standing behind, and every single child was ordered to shoot the man in front of him in the head. Right here, on these same blocks of stone. This theater was for art, not executions.

My heart was on fire.

> *Let it hurt*
> *Let it burn*
> *Let it turn into ashes,*
> *then, blow it away and make space for a new heart to be born*

I felt the souls of the martyrs collected in one, that of my spirit. "I am ready, my lord." And I started moving through space, dragging my feet in the cracks in the rock and stirring up little clouds that followed my movements, like smoke from the burned bodies that had passed through here. The theater itself was dancing with me. My music was the beating of my heart and my breath. I wasn't fleeing from the present, but holding on to it with all the strength I had, like an eagle, fighting the ghosts that haunted this place, dancing in rage, expressing my fears and my mother's suffering.

I caught a glimpse of her during a pirouette—she was sitting on the steps, her hands on her knees as though praying, at the same angle to the stage as when she came to see my first show nine years ago. The one that my father saw on television, when he discovered my clandestine dancing. Back then she had been surrounded by people, but she stood out, thanks to the bright red dress she'd worn for the occasion. This time, she was equally conspicuous, but it was because she was alone and dressed in black, in contrast with the white stone, like a desert rose dried by the horrors of war.

I also briefly glimpsed Roozbeh, the camera on his shoulder, busily recording every precious second. We didn't have much time.

When I finished, we left the theater, and no one felt much like talking. The grim atmosphere had affected our mood, and we were steeped in a tense silence that no one had any intention of breaking. But my mother did, asking us to move into the shade because the sun had burned my skin—I hadn't even noticed. Then she asked if we could stop by her parents' house. She didn't often find herself in Palmyra, free to move through the checkpoints.

The house still stood, but it was severely damaged both outside and inside. The usual atmosphere there no longer surprised me— an atmosphere that contained everything that had passed through here, the good and the bad, all of them influencing the moment and making it so difficult to bear.

My mother was crying. She bent over, collecting what she could—some old photographs and a blanket she'd made for me when I was little. She straightened up and wandered through the completely looted house.

We returned to Damascus. Still no one spoke. I imagined how the next meeting with my mother's family would be, the questions they would ask her about Palmyra and about the house. They would want to hear every detail and then also to see Roozbeh's footage. I thought perhaps it would be best just to show that first. I wondered how my mother would feel when she spoke to her parents, having to bear their tears.

The next day, we went to film my dance class at the SOS Children's Village in Damascus. After that, I invited Roozbeh and Emma to our apartment. Together with my family, we had a farewell dinner for Roozbeh. When Roozbeh left, he had tears in his eyes and gave me a hug. He said, "I wish your life will change for the better."

"Inshallah," I said.

"CAN I USE YOURS, Ram? I haven't been able to switch mine on for two days now."

"Fine, but make sure you don't break mine too."

"I told you it wasn't my fault—it broke itself."

My mother, slightly reluctant, passed me her phone. For two days, I had been trying to get my old phone to work, with no luck. A month had passed since Roozbeh had returned to the Netherlands.

I went straight onto Facebook to see if anyone had been trying to get in touch. There were hundreds of notifications, messages, and friend requests.

"Ram, Ram, look at this!"

"Well, someone's been trying to get in touch with you," she said.

I began opening the messages. Among the people on the top of the list was Roozbeh, with an urgent request for me to phone him.

"Ram? Can I make a call?"

She looked at me as though I was a fool for asking.

"Roozbeh?"

"Ahmad! But what happened? I've been trying to call for days now . . . writing on Facebook, email . . . haven't you seen your emails, Ahmad?"

"No, no, I haven't seen anything. My phone's out of action. What's happened?"

He was laughing.

"What's happened is that the reportage's been released, Ahmad. It's been released and everyone loves it. Everyone loves you. Haven't you noticed how many people are writing to you, how many have seen the rooftop video?"

"I told you, I haven't seen anything."

"And they want to help you. Take a look at the emails. I know there are schools and ballet companies that have written to you; they want you to join them! Even the Dutch National Ballet wants to help you, the company I showed you on the internet when I was there—the Amsterdam Ballet, remember?"

"Of course, of course, I remember." My mother watched me, unsure how to read the expression on my face. "Sorry, can you give me a minute or two just to get my head round all this? I'll call you back."

I tried to explain to my mother what was happening while I browsed through the emails, but I couldn't keep my thoughts straight—my mind was flitting wildly, excited by this news that had come out of the blue. After Roozbeh left, I hadn't thought of him for a while or the adventures we had together, and even less about the reportage.

Yet here it was, in my in-box, a message from the Dutch National Ballet. And it was true—they were asking about me, said they'd like me to dance with them, and offered help with a visa. My hands were shaking as I reread the email. The words became more and more concrete, their meaning expanding and taking possession of the space around me until I found myself completely immersed in another dimension, a dimension consisting of one email and many, many dreams that had been repressed for too long. For a moment I wondered if I was dreaming.

My sister's voice stirred me from my reverie. She was holding out her phone. "It's Dad, for you."

The last thing I needed. "Tell him I'm not here."

"Of course you are. Come on, speak to him."

"But I don't want to!"

"He's your father, Ahmad," my mother said. "You have to speak with him, tell him what's happening."

My mother had spoken. I put the receiver to my ear reluctantly.

"Ahmad! You don't need to explain anything, I know everything. Germany wants you. They've already organized a visa for you to come here—you have to collect it in Lebanon. Come on, Ahmad. Come join me here in Berlin."

"No," I said brusquely.

"What do you mean, no?"

"I don't want to come to you."

"But what are you on about? This is no time for craziness. Come here immediately."

"Listen, I don't want you trying to plan out my life for me again. Just let me get on with things; let me decide on my own."

I gave the phone back to my sister—I could still hear his voice shouting at the other end of the line, and my mother was passing me her phone again.

"It's Roozbeh. He keeps calling; it must be urgent."

"Ahmad," Roozbeh said excitedly. "It's me. Stay on the line, there's someone here who wants to speak to you."

"Hello, Ahmad? It's a pleasure to speak to you. I'm Ted Brandsen. I direct the Dutch National Ballet. First off, I want to compliment your talent and dancing. The news stories about you have had a big impact on all of us. Did you read the email we sent?"

"The email from the ballet? Yes, I read it just now."

"Great! And what do you think?"

"For the moment, I'm having trouble thinking. I'm a bit confused."

"I understand, I understand. Just let me say one thing—we'll do all we can to bring you here. We won't leave you alone."

"But how? I am a stateless person. I have no passport, no way of getting a visa to leave. And no, I don't want to go to Amsterdam as a refugee. Absolutely not."

"You'll see that we'll manage. And then we thought we could get you here on a student visa, not as a refugee. All you have to do is to trust us. Trust us, and we'll take care of it. We'll manage this. You'll see."

"That's very kind of you to try."

I told Ted good-bye and flopped onto the sofa. I gestured to my mother to sit down. I must have gone a bit pale during these last two phone calls, because she was looking at me with a terrified expression.

I put my head on her legs, and she started caressing my hair—the position that calms me most when I'm agitated and have a decision to make. At that moment, however, I didn't feel like making any decisions. I was overwhelmed.

Perhaps she could help me see clearly.

"Ram . . . I have something to tell you."

TEN

TWO MONTHS LATER, in October, as my plane was approaching Amsterdam, I thought of the words my mother said in my ear when she hugged me for the last time before she pushed me into the car that was taking me to Lebanon.

"You will leave me anyway, either to fulfill your dreams or to go to your death in the army. Go, Ahmad, live, follow your dreams, find your home. I'll be here waiting for you."

I wiped my tears and looked out from the window of the airplane. I focused on where I was going. The green surrounding the city below fascinated me.

The moment I stepped onto Dutch soil, I inhaled the air of freedom. Amsterdam. Schiphol Airport. Two in the afternoon. A sign on the wall said "EXIT—No entry beyond this point." As if anyone would turn back.

The sliding doors opened, and the river of people I was part of headed out of the baggage claim area. I carried the suitcase my mother had packed for me when I refused to pack my luggage, as well as an oud in its case and a canvas, which my brother had painted, in a plastic tube.

I still had trouble believing where I was. The signs, in English and Dutch, weren't enough to convince me—I was constantly worried that I might wake up and find it was all a dream. Or something might happen, something that ruined everything with no warning. So many extraordinary things had happened recently that I expected anything.

In the meantime, I let myself be carried along by the united and compact body of the hundreds of people around me—even if I hadn't been able to read English, they would have led me to the exit.

On the other side of the sliding doors was a sea of people, even more people, all standing there with eyes glued to the doors. I knew Roozbeh was among them, coming to meet me. I searched for him in the midst of the unknown faces and recognized him immediately, carrying his big camera on his shoulder as he moved toward me. He had a whole welcoming committee with him. He was surrounded by people, all of them smiling warmly, and there were cameras everywhere. I had a strange premonition—I thought I was going to have to get used to television cameras observing me all the time. I wasn't ready for this. I started shaking, didn't know what to say, how to behave. Before I could think of what to do or say, I heard a man's voice welcoming me—it was Ted Brandsen, the director of the Dutch National Ballet. Then a woman embraced me and whispered, "You're safe now." She introduced herself as Marja.

It must have been the tiredness from the journey, the stress, or the fact that up to this moment I hadn't really understood the extent of what was happening, but I burst into tears. I hugged

Roozbeh and said hello to everyone, even to the lenses pointing at me. I felt loved and wanted, and as Marja had just said, safe—the most difficult sensation to process, as I hadn't felt safe for so long.

We had coffee in an airport café and talked of this and that, about my flight, my future, how I felt. So much to take in, and all so much bigger than me. I responded without really thinking too much.

A gentleman introducing himself as Nicolas Mansfield, director of the Reisopera, put a jacket around my shoulders. I was in short sleeves and sweating, so I told him I didn't need it.

"You'll see soon enough that you need it," he said. He had such a convincing voice, it was hard to say no. And as soon as we got outside, I saw he was right—I was shocked by the cold. A black van with dark windows was waiting for us. Five of us got in, including Roozbeh, and we set off. I was being looked after from the moment of arrival, which was very reassuring.

"We'll take you home now—you'll see; you'll like it. Your housemate is a nice guy and an excellent dancer with our company," Ted Brandsen said. He also offered to let me take some classes. I thanked him. I kept on saying 'thank you' to everyone I met on that day. Everyone seemed happy. Although they were all so friendly, I felt an unbridgeable gap between us.

"After that, we'd like to take you to see the rehearsals for this evening's show."

Straightaway? It was going to be a very long day. I would love to rest for a while and see the city, but I didn't think I should complain.

I looked out the window. I'd have liked some time alone, with everything happening so quickly, and I felt as though I was missing things along the journey. The buildings sped past on the other side of the glass—such colorful buildings, but the dark tint of the glass prevented me from really seeing their detail. "Who lives there?" I wondered. "What are their lives like?"

We arrived. I reached out for the handle, but the door opened automatically. Everyone got out and we went into a building and up the stairs, with the driver behind us. He insisted on carrying my suitcase for me. The apartment was large and well furnished, a dream compared to the living spaces I'd been used to. I met my housemate, a Brazilian named Daniel. He hugged me immediately and kissed me on both cheeks. He seemed like a straightforward and sincere person. He showed me my room, the walls of which were covered with National Ballet posters.

"We'll be in the kitchen. We'll let you sort out your things, and then we'll head to the school."

Together with the others, the television cameras finally moved away. They had followed my every move since I left the airport.

I was ready in only a couple of minutes, as I really had very few things to sort out. I sat on the bed, exhausted; if I'd lain down, I'd have fallen asleep immediately. So I gritted my teeth and faced the day. We got back in the van and headed toward the National Opera House. They spoke to me about laws and norms, forms and procedures, rights and constrictions, but I found it hard to follow what they were saying. I was struggling to keep my eyes open, trying to observe through the van windows the first canals I'd ever seen in my life, people dressed in all sorts of ways out on the streets, the infinity of bicycles overtaking us in traffic.

I kept up this forced wakefulness until we were inside the theater, at the entrance to the rehearsal room, where piano music reawakened my attention. I saw dozens of young dancers, all different nationalities, all sharing a common grace of movement that reminded me of the YouTube videos I used to watch surreptitiously at home. A bolt of electricity ran through my body, making me move, gently imitating the dancers' steps. When the exercise ended, the door opened and a hand pushed me inside.

"Hello! Hi, everybody!"

The words came out of my mouth spontaneously—I didn't know what else to say. Perhaps my voice was too loud; perhaps this wasn't how they did things here; but for the second time since my arrival, I received looks of astonishment. Then applause. It was as though they already knew who I was, as though they knew my story. I sat and watched them continue with the rehearsal. And then the tiredness, rocked by the sweet melody, returned, and I lost all sense of time.

When the rehearsal was over, I said to myself, "Could I now finish for the day and go back to my new home?" No, they had other plans for me—off to eat at the National Ballet canteen, and we had to hurry because the show was beginning soon. I resigned myself to following them wherever they went. So, to the canteen. All I could manage to eat was some rice and boiled potatoes, even though around me were all sorts of dishes—warm and cold, meats of all kinds, foods I didn't even know existed. Everywhere in the canteen, people were eating as though this was their first meal after years of famine, or their last meal ever.

During the meal, although fatigued, I tried to engage myself in conversation with a smile. I realized that my English wasn't advanced enough to convey everything I wanted to say. Before I spoke, I had to think in Arabic, translate mentally into English, and then force myself to pronounce it all in the most understandable way possible. It was, again, exhausting.

After the meal, we were off to the ballet, *La Bayadère*. For the second time on that incredible day, an electric current ran through my body, waking me up and allowing me to concentrate. It must have been the theater—enormous, with a stage that seemed endless, the bright red color of the seats in the auditorium, the music coming live from the orchestra that settled into my bones, the dancers who resonated within my soul. Anna Tsygankova and Daniel Camargo were dancing that evening—two excellent dancers I'd never imagined I would see live. It was all wonderful and all too much at the same time. I was thrilled, I was in tears. Being in the theater was the most unreal moment of the day, the moment that more than any other confused me, prevented me from processing what my new life was making of me.

I could easily believe that once the show was over, I might step outside and find myself on the dusty, deserted roads of Al-Yarmouk. But no, there was a new city out there, different from any I'd known in my life and with no point of reference for me.

After the show, they finally took me home. When I entered the building I felt lighter, but I still struggled to get to sleep. My brain worked furiously through all the new experiences of the last few hours as I stared at the ceiling.

It was past midnight. I'd been invited to classes with the company at nine-thirty the next morning, and all I could think about was why I was here. "Am I really here?" There had to be a reason, an explanation for my presence in this foreign land so far from my home; there had to be something I could do in this place to develop a sense of belonging. Because at that moment, I felt like a guest who just did not fit in. I did not feel I belonged with those free people.

DURING THE FIRST MONTH of my living in Amsterdam, everybody was asking me if I had got used to this new city, but the change was so radical that I knew it would be some time before I reached some kind of normality. Every day I saw new things, I discovered and learned. My English was improving, and I was continually astonished by details that were unimaginable in my culture. But I also still struggled to find my place in this new world. Everything around me seemed unreal. I felt that I had become a little orphan child who had to learn all about this life alone, scared of everybody, as if every person I met wanted a piece of me. I got lost many times in Amsterdam's semicircular streets; the rain mixed with the tears on my face, hiding them from the strangers. "Who is the stranger? Me? Or them?"

I was saying yes to everything. Every part I was asked to film to continue the television reportage with Roozbeh, every interview I was asked to do, every performance I was asked to participate in, every person I was asked to meet. I was just doing what I was asked, because I was so scared that saying no would send me back to Syria. I often would hide myself in the underground garage of the building and dance there, sweating out my tears. Then I would go back to the life I had to deal with, the life where some people called me a hero and others called me a "Middle Eastern media freak."

But all these challenges were outside the dance studio, where I spent most of my time. I felt at ease there. The Dutch National Ballet was rehearsing for its premiere of *Coppélia,* in which I was cast in the role of a priest. This was going to be my first stage performance in Europe.

One evening, as we finished our rehearsal and we were getting ready to go out to dinner, Daniel said to me, buttoning the shirt he'd brought for the occasion, "You paid last time; this time let us pay."

"It was the least I could do—you were all so kind to invite me out with you," I said.

"Someone has to show you the town. And the life we live here. It's easy to lose yourself in Amsterdam."

Joey, one of Daniel's friends and now a friend of mine as well, came up to us. He was still in his dance clothes.

"You're not changed yet?" Daniel said. "Come on, we've booked the table."

"Sorry, I've just finished my rehearsal," Joey responded to Daniel and then said to me, "Hey, Ahmad, have you heard who's up in the studio?"

"No. Who?"

Joey smiled meaningfully. "Have I missed something?" I wondered.

"If I tell you, you will be running," he said and started laughing.

"Oh, come on then, tell us."

"Roberto Bolle."

The world suddenly stopped turning; I almost fell to the floor.

"Are you serious?"

"Sure, he's rehearsing. He's up there in Studio 2, rehearsing with Anna Tsygankova."

To think that Roberto Bolle was in the building, in this building at that moment, was unreal. He had never been anything more than a moving image for me, an ideal way above any other ideal, an ideal toward which I strove with all my strength. He had been all that, but abstractly—he had never been a physical body occupying space in a given moment. And, above all, he'd never been this close to me. My new friends smiled at me.

"And what do I do now?" I said.

"What do you mean? You go up and see him!"

"And the restaurant . . . the booking?"

Daniel looked at me seriously. "Get a move on, or I'll send you up there with a kick in the butt."

I left the dressing room running and took the stairs two at a time. My hands were clammy and I was sweating. Before me was a door, and behind it was the realization of a life's dream and, paradoxically, the end of a dream, the unknown that arrives once a dream comes true. But my experience in Amsterdam couldn't be reduced to what I knew so far; there had to be more. Maybe it was behind that door. I opened it.

Bolle was on his own, doing stretching exercises on the floor. He looked as I'd expected him to and as I'd known him from videos, but at the same time he was different, even though I couldn't say how. He was certainly more handsome. As soon as he saw me, he stood up and came toward me.

"Is Anna here?" I asked, my voice trembling, pretending I had come to see her.

"No, she left five minutes ago," he said, placing his hand elegantly on the barre. I realized that I didn't know his voice—it was different from the recorded voice in the internet interviews; much more stable, reassuring in a certain way.

I moved forward and put my hand on the barre too. I couldn't stop looking at him, but I couldn't find anything to say.

"But you . . . "

He looked me over. "You're not the Syrian dancer, are you?"

"You know me?"

My internal voice screamed, "Bolle knows who I am, he knows I exist!" The rehearsal room, together with the entire world, was suddenly topsy-turvy.

"Of course, Anna told me about you. In fact, a lot of people have spoken to me about you. I'm Roberto. Pleased to meet you."

He held out his hand, even more elegant as he let go of the barre.

There was something about him, a sort of energy around him, a magnetic field that attracted everything in the room toward him, me included. He was full of his spirit. I stepped tentatively closer and shook his hand. Everything happened in slow motion. The expression on my face was probably absurd. I didn't know if I'd gone red with shyness, but I felt hot, and I was sweating more than ever. I was full of my spirit.

"So, to what do I owe this visit? What is this aura of mystery and excitement that goes before you?" he asked with a smile.

"I don't know . . . maybe it's because I come from far away."

"From where?"

"From Damascus."

His expression changed; he became more reflective. Perhaps I shouldn't have started this conversation. I mean, I didn't *really* know him, I had no idea what he thought of people like me. "But he cannot be anything but wonderful—he dances so divinely. I can feel his spirit," I said to myself.

"And why have you come here, if I may ask?"

I could hear from his voice that he was sincerely interested; he wanted to know about me and my story, to really get to know me. I was certain of this. I felt I could trust him; I couldn't resist him. And then, after all those years spent following him, I did feel as though I knew him in a way.

I gave him an outline of my story, of my adventure that began with watching his video hidden away in my room as a boy and had brought me to that precise place at that precise moment from a war-torn country. It was as if a circle was closing, the scattered pieces coming together. Many things seemed clearer. Everything, from the most insignificant to the most painful detail of my life, made sense in the light of this meeting.

I finished my story. I had no idea how long I'd spoken, but what I said must have been enough for Bolle to understand me, or at least to have an idea about me. I could see that he was touched, even worried, sometimes surprised; at some moments sad, at others happy. Now he was silent, deep in thought, with his eyes turned to the floor. Then he looked at me intensely and said, "I must compliment you. From what you've told me, which I imagine isn't even everything, I see that you have the gift of a rare strength, something truly difficult to find. Perhaps you're not aware of it, but you have something special in you."

We smiled, both almost embarrassed by the strong, natural rapport we felt with each other. We hugged. Our spirits hugged each other.

We left the rehearsal room, and while I walked with him to the dressing room, he said, "Listen, how about we meet up again tomorrow? You can come and watch the rehearsals."

Well, I accepted his invitation. "Of course. I would love that. See you tomorrow then."

We said good-bye.

I went down the stairs at a run, two steps at a time, as excited as a little boy at the idea of recounting my meeting to my friends and going back through it in every detail. And I was sure that I was going to have trouble falling asleep that night.

The next day I watched Roberto rehearsing a new dance. I had difficulty believing what I was seeing: even Roberto Bolle had to repeat a movement several times before perfecting it. Whatever he did, he did well, but the first time didn't quite work for him. Then he would try again, and again, each time improving the movement. For some movements, he repeated it as many as twelve times.

The hours spent watching him working through his doubts, repeating and in the end succeeding, made my impression of him more human, which made me feel closer to him. And it was motivating for me—it showed me that even the greatest artists, who seem so perfect to us by their very nature, have to work to achieve the results they offer the world. I felt like going into a rehearsal room right away to practice, perhaps try something new or perhaps just dance on my own and push myself to the farthest possible limits, challenging myself to become better. I knew I had a long road ahead of me, but these hours made it look a bit less steep.

And then Roberto invited me out to dinner! We were out on the street after rehearsal, the cold wind having no effect on the pleasure this walk gave me, the darkness protecting us from the gaze of the world, giving me the sensation of living through an intense moment of peace, a moment that felt like mine for the first time since I arrived in Amsterdam.

"What do you want to eat?" he asked me.

"I don't know. Whatever you prefer."

"Do you like fish?"

"Of course!"

"Seafood it is," he said.

We wandered around for a few more minutes, found a fish restaurant, and went inside. Bolle suggested that we order lots of different dishes to share. I observed and tried to memorize every single gesture he made, especially this latest one: eating from the same plate, which was something we do only with family or close friends in my culture, and which showed me that the person sitting opposite me was open, humble, and above all genuine, not hiding behind an artificial wall of fake friendliness. This made me relaxed, being with this accomplished person without any sense of pressure.

As we ate, Bolle was full of questions. He wanted to know everything, down to the tiniest detail. He asked me where I was living, asked me to describe the building and the people who lived in it, he asked me about Al-Yarmouk, about what it was like to live in the neighborhood and its history. He wanted to know what led me to become involved in dancing for the first time, and I told him about that magical vision of *Swan Lake* that happened almost by pure chance. In describing that moment to him, I realized how providential it was. I wondered how my life would have worked out if I hadn't looked around that door.

Then he asked me about my training, about the companies I'd worked in, the shows I'd danced in, and about the war and how I managed to combine the conflict with my dancing. I told him about my basement school, the kids I taught, the Lebanese television show, all the shows I performed around the Arab world, the problems and the satisfactions that came with them. I told him how dancing saved my life several times, including the time in the shelter during the bombing—how wanting to get to the rehearsal at all costs saved not only my life and Saeed's but also the lives of dozens of other people.

"I can't even imagine myself in a situation like that. I don't think I would have survived," he said.

"Of course you would have survived; surviving is part of being human. And it's true for everyone—we're all suited by nature to surviving at any cost."

He fell back in his chair and folded his arms. "You're probably right," he said, almost to himself. "But let's change the subject. Have you got yourself an agent?"

"Yes, I have . . . but I'm not too happy with the way it's working."

"How come?"

"Because I've noticed that whenever people ask me directly to work with them, then everything goes well. I manage to get some appreciation on the basis of my personality. Deep down, I'm a very simple person. When things go through my agent, people aren't so happy and they're less interested. I just like having straightforward and direct contact with people."

"I see. Then let me give you some advice, Ahmad," he said. "It's extremely important that you have an agent you can trust. Do you know what I did?"

"What?"

"I put myself in my sister's hands. She's been my agent for years."

"Really? But is she a professional agent?"

"She is now. And we work very well together, because there's a trusting relationship between us."

His sister. He was right; I needed to find someone I could trust blindly. Someone who'd help me and want to embark on this journey together, and who wasn't simply using me to profit from my work or my story.

"After which, let me give you another piece of advice. May I?"

"Of course!"

"Good. As you'll have noticed, this city is a rather particular place. It's a bit as though it were a city full of . . . candy, let's say. Are you following me?"

"I think so." I was a bit puzzled.

"Well, there's this candy everywhere, and the more there is, the more you have to be careful. You must remain concentrated on your objective. Never miss a dance class, don't let your body relax too much, or your mind. I mean, don't let the things you see around you choke you."

I listened to him closely, ignoring the food on my plate. I didn't want to miss a word.

"And be careful how you present yourself to the public and to those who may be interested in working with you. Your body is your instrument; take care of it and don't abuse it. And then there's social media," he added with a smile.

I smiled too. I was present on social media. I enjoyed it as an experience. I knew the same was true for him because I followed him on all the platforms.

"Social media can help, there's no doubt about that, but they can also prove to be a danger for your image. Above all, you need a good press officer with you, one you trust, obviously. Then you need a website. Do you have one?"

"No."

"Create one. As for the profiles on the networks that you already use, you have to understand that they're no longer private but public, and for this reason you have to keep them as professional as possible."

Dinner went on in the same vein, even more relaxed. We made small talk; I asked him some questions and learned some of the background to his dancing life that I never could have imagined from videos on the internet. As we finished dinner and were about to get up to leave, he gestured to me to remain sitting for a moment. "Please know," he said, "that you can count on me. Whatever happens, whatever you need, don't hesitate to call me. I'll be able to give you a hand, and I want to do it, no matter what it may be about. I promise you, I'll do all I can to help you."

We left the restaurant and headed toward his hotel in silence, each in his own thoughts. We stopped once or twice to look at the tired canals, with the colored lights of Amsterdam reflected in them. In front of the hotel, we hugged each other.

"Inshallah."

"Inshallah," he answered and added, "Have you ever heard Sting's song? The one with that title?"

"No."

"You should listen to it; it's beautiful. Do you know his music?"

"Of course. I used a track of his 'Desert Rose' for my audition for the television show."

Bolle laughed and said, "You see? Nothing happens by chance."

ELEVEN

OVER THAT WINTER, I still struggled to orient myself in Amsterdam. As in Damascus, I was using a bicycle for transportation. Marja gave me one. The roads were so busy that I was easily carried away by the flow of the traffic. When it happened, it gave me a chance to see as much of the city as I could on my bike, to look around and enjoy what I saw. Every day I discovered something new, and those images of Amsterdam fed my brain. People were so free, dressing the way they wanted, behaving as they liked, loving whomever they wished without worrying about the opinions of others. Passersby minded their own business, making no judgments. I felt great excitement at these changes—great joy, to be honest—and I wanted to explore as much as I could, though that wasn't possible with my schedule.

I was working intensively on dancing. Some days I took two ballet classes, one with the company and another one with the ballet school, as well as doing rehearsals for *Coppélia*. I appeared in all the *Coppélia* performances, and some days I performed twice. I pushed myself hard, wanting to feel that I deserved the opportunity given to me. At the same time, it troubled me to think that I had left the people who meant so much to me, who didn't deserve to be abandoned. I was fine: I ate at least three meals a day, I went out, I enjoyed myself. But what right did I have to all this? Why me and not someone else? I felt guilty being happy. And I was looking forward to the time when I could start supporting my family financially.

But there was something else that made my heart heavy: my father. I knew he was staying in a camp for asylum-seekers in Berlin. We had not been father and son for eleven years. But I wanted to break through the wall between us and start a new relationship, because I wanted to start my new life in Europe from scratch, leaving all the hatred we had in Syria behind.

When I had the chance, I traveled to Berlin to visit him. Roozbeh accompanied me with his camera. I had no idea how my visit would go until the moment I saw my father at the camp, a building with a huge hall that was divided into compartments. When he saw me coming into his compartment, he jumped toward me and embraced me. We started crying, forgetting the presence of the camera. When we calmed down, he said, "At first I was against it, but you have proven yourself. You have chosen your own path and come very far. I respect you, my son." Finally, he could see my truth, and I could hug him after all those years. I went with him to visit my little half-sisters at the apartment where they were living with their mother. My half-sisters told me they loved watching my dance videos on YouTube and asked me cute questions about the videos. We were happy to see each other.

On the way back to Amsterdam, I felt lighter. Forgiveness was the key to freedom from the chains of hatred.

Soon afterward, I spoke to my mother on WhatsApp.

"Ahmad, how are you?"

"Hi, Ram. Everything's fine, and you?"

She was as beautiful as ever, even though the image quality wasn't great. Only when I saw her did I realize how much I missed her. The reassuring tone of her voice, her long blond hair, the way she looked at me. I missed everything about her.

"Fine. Let's say we're getting there."

"What do you mean? Problems?"

"No, don't worry. Tell me about you. What are you up to these days?"

"I'm dancing a lot. I spend all day at the National Academy in classes with teachers who come from all over the world, and I work with the company. Guess who I met a few weeks ago?"

"Who? Someone I know?"

I told her about my meeting with Roberto Bolle.

"Really? But that's wonderful; I'm very happy for you. Was it exciting? What's he like in real life?"

"Incredible. The way he moves, the way he speaks. The spirit of dance must have given him a part of itself. He's special—you'd have to meet him to understand fully."

"Well, I'm sure this spirit of dance must have given part of itself to you too. I'm so happy you could meet him. Tell me about the dance company. What's it like there? Have you made friends?"

"Well . . . I've told you about Giovanni and Daniel, the guys I share the apartment with. They are nice. Daniel and I have a lot of things in common. He's from Brazil. That's why we understand each other when we talk about home. And Giovanni is from Italy. I don't know the others in the company very well."

"And apart from home and the company, how's it going?"

"One thing that's going on is that people sometimes recognize me in the street."

"So you've become something of a star?"

"No, not really a star, but when they stop me, it can be a bit of a pain—they ask me nosy questions."

"Ah! Things really have changed for you. But listen: only you can hear your inner voice. Nobody else can know what is in your mind or who you really are, so make sure to stay connected to yourself and listen, observe, and learn."

"Of course, Ram. Every time I get lost, I go back to my roots."

My mother looked sad, though she tried to hide it. I knew perfectly well why, but it was difficult for me to bring up the subject.

"But how are things going there, Ram?"

"I told you, everything's fine."

"No, really. Tell me about the situation."

She paused for a moment, looked around, took a deep breath, and said, "What can I say? Things haven't improved. There's no point my describing it; you know what I'm talking about. What has changed is that things are more difficult for the routine stuff—electricity is available only four hours a day, we hardly get water, and the price of food goes up every day. At least here in Al-Tadamon we're relatively safe."

While she was speaking, I'd felt a bit hungry and reached for the fruit bowl next to me. But I stopped myself in time. I put the banana I'd taken hold of back in the bowl and pushed it away. I should not eat during calls with my mother; I had to remember that.

"Ram, I'm working here with the company and I'm earning some money. I will send some to you."

"No, Ahmad, don't you worry about us—your money is yours, for your future. Keep it, and we'll get by one way or another."

"One day, I will buy you a house as I promised you."

"Inshallah."

She would never accept any help; she was too proud. I would have to send her money through her brother without telling her.

"All right. Though I'd really like to see you again one day. Here's a kiss, Ram."

"A kiss for you too, Ahmad. Take care."

This conversation, and others like it, ended suddenly, leaving the atmosphere in the room even worse than it had been during the call. The motionless screen left room for all sorts of thoughts, and I found myself imagining the worst.

THAT EVENTFUL YEAR finally came to an end. It was New Year's Eve, three months since my arrival in Amsterdam. We were getting ready to go to a party at Priscilla's; she was a friend of Daniel's, also Brazilian, from the company. Everyone had to bring something to eat from their national cuisine, and I had offered to bring dessert.

"What have you made?"

"It's a secret—that's why it's hidden under the foil."

We went downstairs to the waiting Uber. We must have looked funny with our heavy jackets and food containers in our hands, but winter was hard going for both of us. Perhaps even more so for him. We got in the car and headed off to the party.

I was nervous. New Year's seemed to be an important celebration in Amsterdam, but it was my first. I was tempted to stay at home, but Daniel never would have allowed that. He must have noticed something, though, because he took my hand and said, "Listen, keep calm. You'll have fun."

"Thanks. But how should I behave? What do I have to do when I arrive?"

"Oh, these questions. Just be yourself and everything will be fine. They're all really cool people—no judgments, no expectations. Just let things flow naturally, and don't try to be anyone other than yourself."

I was so glad to know Daniel. Without him, it would all have been more difficult for me. I liked his ability to be at ease in any situation and not let himself be fazed by social anxiety. For me, this was still a problem because this society was too different from the one I came from. I was always worried about offending someone or behaving badly. But I was working on it day by day, party by party.

"Here we are. Have a good evening and a Happy New Year!" Daniel said to the driver. "Come on, Ahmad, what are you waiting for? Let's go."

Daniel held the door to the building open for me; I slipped in, and he closed it quickly behind me. I let him lead the way, and we started up the stairs.

"I think it's this apartment."

"Isn't it best if you phone her before . . . "

"Priscilla!"

"Daniel! Ahmad! Welcome. Come in, quickly. Don't let the heat out, or the cold in. How are you guys?"

Priscilla hugged me and kissed both cheeks. I tried to be spontaneous and comfortable, but it was as though I were stuck in the doorway.

"Give that to me and I'll put it in the fridge. What is this wonderful thing you've made?" she asked as she took the big bowl from my hands.

"It's a rice dessert, with milk and coconut."

"Really? Did you hear that, Daniel? We have that in Brazil too . . . that's great!" Priscilla said, peeking under the foil. Who would ever have thought that Brazil and Syria would have the same dessert?

I watched her go along the corridor, arm in arm with Daniel, as I hung up my jacket. They were both fantastic—such extroverts and always full of life. I went into the living room. There were a dozen or so people; the atmosphere was relaxed. I said hello to everyone, and they smiled back. The wall on the opposite side of the room had lots of photographs—not of Priscilla but of her guests. I found mine immediately—four of them, taken from Facebook—one with my mother, one with the Enana company, one with the class at the institute, and one with Saeed.

"Do you like it?" Priscilla said, coming in behind me. "I did one for each of you; I wanted us all to feel a bit more at home this evening. And I wanted it to be a surprise, so I didn't tell anyone."

I was so astonished that I didn't know what to say. I took her arm and said a feeble "Thank you." Over her shoulder, I saw Daniel smiling to me from across the room.

We danced to a lot of Brazilian music, but I had my moment when I was asked to put Syrian music on, which everyone liked. We took turns showing the traditional dances of our countries, holding one another's hands and hugging each other. It was as if the room itself were spinning, not us.

"Come on, let's go outside!" someone shouted. "Let's go see the fireworks."

I was happy to be getting outside, and I was the first one out the door. The cold air against my sweat-drenched face refreshed me and cleared my mind. All around me, people were embracing, exchanging love because they had so much love to give, looking in the same direction as though waiting for something. Their eyes shone and shimmered, like stars in the sky.

This pleasant vision literally exploded. A hissing whistle that seemed to come from inside my head. Then a boom so loud it shook me to my bones. A flash, another whistle, another boom, and yet another flash. I had to take cover immediately—the glass in the windows might explode any second. The whistling got louder; they were getting closer. I felt my blood pulsing, rushing through my veins, and my eyes were bulging, as though trying to come out of my head. Another boom—it must have fallen very close to us. I was having trouble breathing; I could feel the dust scratching at my throat and blocking my lungs. Around me, people were running, panicking, afraid for their lives, crushing me so I couldn't move. The ground shook, the air shook, my legs shook, and I crouched down so as not to collapse.

I pulled my legs to my chest and put my head between my knees. I closed my eyes but then saw it even more clearly—the dirty yellow roads, the men dressed in black, the gray buildings, the dark red spray that skittered everywhere and soiled everything, the pieces of torn flesh rolling in front of me. I saw women throw themselves to the ground as they screamed, scratching at their faces before the burned bodies. I saw flames licking the sides of a car in the silence before the explosion, the people staggering as the shock wave hit, all covered in white ash and detritus as they wandered aimlessly. In the background were the whistling and booms of the bombs, the mortar shells falling on buildings and obliterating them. They had captured me; they wanted to take me away, they wanted to kill me, to throw me into a mass grave. My mother was screaming my name. The name of my grandfather.

"Ahmad, Ahmad, it's me, Daniel! Look at me, please look at me."

I opened my eyes. I was outside, sitting on the ground. The bombing had stopped. Daniel was next to me, shaking my arm.

"It was fireworks, Ahmad. Calm down now; you're still shaking."

It was fireworks. But what I had seen was something else. I was sure of it.

"Daniel? Where am I?"

"You're in Amsterdam; you're safe. I promise you."

My head spun, my belly ached, and I felt nauseated. I wanted to sleep. I wanted to go home.

"Can we get out of here, Daniel?"

"Yes. The Uber is already on its way."

He stroked my head, pulling it to his shoulder. I closed my eyes again. Darkness, a silent and eternal blackness.

The next afternoon, New Year's Day. The clock on the bedside table read two in the afternoon. Or at least I think it did—I was having trouble focusing. I tried to get out of bed, but I fell backward immediately. My head was pounding.

Confused images from the previous night began to take shape—Priscilla's party, the photographs on the wall, the apartment—and then I remembered, all of a sudden, the fireworks that in my head had turned into bombs, the shouts of joy that became cries of desperation, the New Year's wishes that became prayers. Fear had made me see things that didn't exist. Or rather, things that had existed, things that were impressed in my mind and would never leave me.

I dragged myself with difficulty to the bathroom, turned on the faucet, and let the water run until it was really cold. I washed my hands, and then I threw water on my face as I rubbed my eyes, my aching jaw, the back of my neck. At last, the headache seemed to recede.

I looked at myself in the mirror and I wondered how the past and present had become so mixed up last night. How could I possibly have believed in all that? To the point of having a panic attack? I thought I'd left all that horror behind me; I hoped I'd never have to meet it again. Instead it returned to find me.

They say time heals all. To which I answer: Time will tell . . .

TWELVE

AFTER THE LAST PERFORMANCE of *Coppélia* with the Dutch National Ballet in January 2017, my life as a professional grew. I received invitations to perform all over Europe and farther afield: not only the Netherlands, but Norway, Italy, Switzerland, France, Spain, Denmark, Belgium, Austria, the United Arab Emirates, and even the United States, although I was still a stateless refugee.

And so I continue. Art is my identity. Dance is my passport.

For each performance, I connect to my spirit to go on stage, where I let my body scream, expressing what I can't say in words, being in my most vulnerable state, putting my heart out there, so open. I never care for applause or a compliment—I am just me, surrendering to my destiny.

It's dance or die.

Dear Mom,

I'm writing to you from the Vondelpark in Amsterdam. I'm sitting on a bench watching people walking with their families, some strolling with those they're in love with, or even just walking with their dogs.

There's a mother over there in front of me. She looks like you in the way she sits and gazes at her son. I'd like to speak to her, but I think she'd be frightened if a stranger with a beard and dark hair were to approach her. It's no surprise, Mom. I'm not surprised by it anymore.

I'd love to be able to see you again, to walk together in this beautiful park, watching the passersby. Coming from a country devastated by a war, both of us would be thinking that some of the people here do not realize how wonderful their world is. I'd like to take you to the Van Gogh museum, just as you've always dreamed of doing, and I'd like to make your dream of a gondola trip in Venice come true, and visiting the theaters in Rome.

Do you remember when I used to dance in my room by candlelight? With Enigma playing so loud?

Do you remember that little kid? I am still him, and you are still the only one who can understand me.

Mom, I miss you.

I miss my family, my friends, my students, and even my tent up on the roof.

I miss breathing the air of Damascus and playing in the sun with the sand in Palmyra.

Mom, I just want to say "I'm sorry."

I'm sorry for leaving you behind. You told me to leave, to follow my dreams, to live, to find my home, to be with people who can understand me. You knew that I didn't belong there. But where do I belong, Mom?

Dance or Die

I flew so high
I crossed mountains and oceans
I cuddled the clouds and I danced through them
I washed my wounds in the waterfalls and I found heaven
in the woods.
I've danced all the dead, every person I've lost.
Who is going to dance me?

I lived my dreams, and I found shelter in the arms of Jochem, who became my soft place to fall and my safe place to hide.

When I left Syria, we both thought my war ended. But no, my war continues.

I wish I could cry in your arms, and hear your voice whispering in my ear to tell me how strong I am, reminding me that I can and I must go on.

I'll go on. I'll do it for you. I'll do it for my grandfather, who asked me to die on my own two feet with my head held high, without ever bowing.

I will go on for all the stateless people, my people, proving to the world that we, stateless, are human beings, who deserve opportunities and rights to live, to be safe, to have homes, and to be successful. I will go on as a voice for those who are still longing for freedom and respect. And I will do it for every kid who needs to be safe and protected.

Mom, so much has happened since you saw me dance at the Roman Theatre in Palmyra . . . the last artist to perform on that stage before it was bombed.

I've danced "Inshallah" with Roberto Bolle to Sting's live music. I represented refugees by dancing "Sacrifice" at the European Parliament on the United Nations World Refugee Day. My body shouted for freedom, dancing to "My Word Is Free" by Emel Mathlouthi at the UNHCR Nansen Refugee Award ceremony. I represented Syrian artists by dancing

"One in a Million" at Ballet Beyond Borders in the United States. And I stand up for kids in my engagements for SOS Children's Villages as their International Friend.

This is my mission. I will take this path, carrying my wounds with pride until the word "stateless" doesn't exist in this world.

My fire is still burning more and more, lighting up my path.

It warms my heart that Saeed is coming here to be by my side, as we promised each other years ago. That makes me happy. But what makes me happier than anything else is that I have kept my promise for you too, by buying a house for you.

"I don't want to fall in love; I want to rise in love." I want to live my life protecting the love I have.

I don't know if we'll see each other again one day, I don't even know what tomorrow may bring. What I do know is that today I am the person I have always wanted to be, and it was all worth my pain.

I love you, Mom; I am proud of carrying your blood in my veins.

Be safe, Mom.

Your son,

Ahmad

ON OCTOBER 13, 2020, I marked the fourth anniversary of my arrival in Amsterdam. Four years ago I left my home, family, and friends and came here, to Europe, dazzled by the cameras that captured every detail of my journey. As soon as I arrived I started working, so hard that I scarcely noticed the profound culture shock of this great change in my life. Yet I know that my time in Europe has helped me grow immensely. So much has happened, and I am so fortunate to have been allowed to reach a level of success, artistically and personally, that I once only dreamed of.

Of course, I have been supported by so many—here in Europe and back home in Syria—and I thank all those people who have believed in me as a person and as an artist. I would like to finish my story by saying to all immigrants who face the challenges I have faced that *arrival is not the solution. Integration is respect.* So be aware of the culture shock, hear yourself, support and protect yourself, try to understand and help yourself to grow. Open your mind and accept the change.

Let's all respect each other and live in peace.

Ahmad Joudeh

I keep searching for home . . .

ACKNOWLEDGMENTS

Thanks to: My grandfather, Ahmad Joudeh: may his spirit
stay in peace, guiding me with his wisdom

My mother and my family

Saeed Akkad and his family

Jochem Van Berne

Roberto Bolle

The Dutch National Ballet

The support group Dance or Die

Marja Delfos

Hitomi Shibuya

Roozbeh Kaboly

Alvise Pirovano

My Italian publisher, DeA Planeta Libri

My American publisher, Imagine Books

People who are supporting me all over the world

All the resistance on my path, which makes me
more persistent to succeed

SOS CHILDREN'S VILLAGES

SOS CHILDREN'S VILLAGES is an international nongovernmental organization that provides humanitarian and developmental assistance to children throughout the world. Founded in Austria in 1949, the organization is set up to protect the rights and interests of children who were orphaned or neglected after World War II. Today, SOS Children's Villages is active in more than 130 countries and territories worldwide.

SOS Children's Villages brings children of different ages and backgrounds together to live in a house with a full-time (parental) caregiver, and there are usually six to fifteen houses in a typical SOS Children's Village. The organization also runs programs to support socially disadvantaged and impoverished families and funds schools, youth centers, and emergency response relief operations around the world. Millions of children and adults benefit from these services and programs.

Many governments and institutions contribute to the SOS Children's Villages programs, but they also depend on private donations. If you are interested in donating to this very worthy cause, visit the SOS Children's Villages website at https://www. sos-usa.org/. There you will also learn about other ways of contributing, including sponsorships, partnerships, and volunteer opportunities.

AHMAD'S WORK RELATED TO THE UNITED NATIONS

UNHRC Nansen Refugee Award

The UN Refugee Agency, UNHCR, honors individuals, groups, and organizations who go above and beyond the call of duty to protect refugees, displaced, and stateless people. Established in 1954, the award celebrates the legacy of Fridtjof Nansen, a Norwegian scientist, polar explorer, diplomat, and first high commissioner for refugees for the League of Nations.

In 2018, Dr. Evan Atar Adaha received the award for his extraordinary dedication as the only surgeon at Maban Referral Hospital, a 120-bed and two-theater facility in Bunj, in the southeastern corner of South Sudan's Upper Nile State. At the ceremony in Geneva, actress Cate Blanchett, a UNHCR Goodwill Ambassador, gave the keynote speech. I was honored to be invited to perform my own choreography for "My Word Is Free," a powerful plea for social justice and a better world by the wonderful Tunisian singer-songwriter Emel Mathlouthi.

United Nation World Refugee Day

World Refugee Day is an international day designated by the United Nations to honor refugees around the globe. It falls each year on June 20 and celebrates the strength and courage of people who have been forced to flee their home country to escape conflict or persecution. World Refugee Day is an occasion to build empathy and understanding for their plight and to recognize their resilience in rebuilding their lives.

In 2018, the European Parliament hosted an event for which I performed my choreography "Sacrifice," expressing my prayer for Syria.

World Press Freedom Conference

The World Press Freedom Conference 2020 was hosted on December 9, 2020, by the United Nations Educational, Scientific and Cultural Organization (UNESCO) and the Kingdom of the Netherlands. Because of the COVID pandemic, the major part of the conference was held online with World Forum in The Hague as the key station. I had the honor to perform "One in a Million," choreographed in collaboration with Robin van Zutphen, at the opening session.

THE DANCE FOR PEACE FUND

AFTER SEEING THE TV reportage about my life in Syria by Roozbeh Kaboly in August 2016, Ted Brandsen, the director of the Dutch National Ballet, established the Dance for Peace Fund together with his colleagues and other individuals. The fund made it possible for me to move to Amsterdam in October 2016 and supported my living and studying in the initial phase of my life in Europe.

2006–2016

Performed as a main dancer for Enana Dance Theater and Ornina Arts Events at major theaters in the Arab world, including Algeria, Bahrain, Jordan, Lebanon, Oman, Qatar, Syria, Tunisia, and United Arab Emirates

2016

The role of priest in *Coppélia*, the Dutch National Ballet, Amsterdam, the Netherlands

2014

Quarterfinalist in the Arabic version of *So You Think You Can Dance*, Beirut, Lebanon

2014–2016

Supported children with challenges by holding dance workshops and shows for children with Down syndrome and for children orphaned by the civil war at SOS Children's Villages Syria

2017

Solo performance "One in a Million" at Gala Internazionale di Danza "Hommage a Marika Besobrasova" e ricordo del Moby Prince, Livorno, Italy

Solo performance "Dance or Die" accompanied by SANGA and The Sankofa Unit, Trocadéro, Paris, France

Principal dancer in GRENZE (N) LOOS, Amsterdam, the Netherlands

Solo performance "Sacrifice" for Geneva Call, Geneva, Switzerland

Solo performance "The Phoenix" in a show with the Dutch National Ballet at Het Concert Gebouw, Amsterdam

Charity shows with SOS Children's Villages, the Netherlands, to support Syrian refugee children in Lebanon, including collaboration with Amsterdam DJ Martin Garrix

TIMELINE (2018–2020)

2018

Duet "Inshallah" with Roberto Bolle with live music of Sting in the television show "Roberto Bolle — Danza con me," Rai 1, Italy

Principal role in Silk Road, Ornina Arts Events, Dubai, United Arab Emirates

Premiere of documentary film *Dance Or Die* by Roozbeh Kaboly, Amsterdam

Solo performance "One in a Million", Danish Royal Theater, Copenhagen, Denmark

TedX Vicenza, Italy

Solo performance "Sacrifice" on UN World Refugee Day, European Parliament, Brussels, Belgium

Solo performance "My Word Is Free" at UNHCR Nansen Refugee Award ceremony, Geneva, Switzerland
Publication of *Danza O Muori* (Dance or Die) by DeA Planeta Libri, Italy

Workshop for the children and youth of SOS Children's Villages Italy, Vicenza, Italy

Principal dancer at Dance4Life, a charity show of SOS Children's Villages Italy, Milan, Italy

2019

Principal dancer in the play *Lik og del* (Like and Share), Kilden Teater og Konserthus, Kristiansand, Norway

International Emmy® Award (Arts Programming) for documentary *Dance Or Die* by Roozbeh Kaboly, New York, USA

Appointed as "International Friend" by SOS Children's Villages International

2020

Solo performance "One in a Million" and member of the jury at Ballet Beyond Borders, Montana, USA

Solo performance "One in a Million," the Dutch National Ballet, Amsterdam

Solo performance "Ya Malikan" with live music of Midist/Wasim in a television charity show in support of the citizens of Beirut; Amsterdam

Video projects during the COVID-19 pandemic:

- E M E L–Kelmti Horra (My Word Is Free)–Quarantine Session

- 100 United Nations World Days

- Video workshop for SOS Children's Villages Italy

Member of the jury panel for the 2020 JCS International Young Creatives Awards of the International Academy of Television Arts & Sciences (International Emmy®)

Solo performance "One in a Million" at the opening session of World Press Freedom Conference 2020, The Hague, the Netherlands, hosted by the United Nations Educational, Scientific and Cultural Organization (UNESCO) and the Kingdom of the Netherlands

SOCIAL MEDIA

WEBSITE: www.ahmadjoudeh.com

INSTAGRAM: @ahmadjoudehofficial

FACEBOOK: @ahmadjoudehofficial

YOUTUBE: Ahmad Joudeh
(https://www.youtube.com/channel/UCGelopUELmagDjnNSDaVLMA)